*Photo by Zel Bowers*

*"...I gravitate to the earthy colors and textures,
trying to let the media show me what it wants to be rather
than forcing it into something.*
*- CINDY HARDIN*

88888888888888888888888888888888888888888888888888888888888888888888
Cover/Artwork Credits ~
Front Cover:  "Dyke in the Doorway" from lesbian images by ana r.
kissed, photographer (biography p. 68).
Back Cover:  From the collection of photography by Lisa M. Wright, from
her card collection, Imagine Images (biography p. 219).
Page i:  "Woman's Face" from the collection of original clay and pottery
by Cindy Hardin (biography p. 194).
Below:  "Womyn of the Moon" a series of prints and woodcuts by Jacque
Harper.  Jacque and 12-year partner, Ruth Brose, offer their collection at
womyn-fests nationally.  "These works show the power and beauty that
Mother Earth has given us."  Catalog: HC 73, Box 129, Drury, Mo. 65638.
Page 1:  "For Lesbian Eyes" Sculpture:  Myriam Fougère, artist, co-
organizer of East (and West) Coast Lesbian Festival.  Her dedication has
reached womyn from all parts of the globe.  Currently resides in Canada.
Photos by Monique Frugier of Philadelphia from her card collection:
MONAR Cards.  Drawing p. 240 - Dawn D. Manna Productions, Florida.
88888888888888888888888888888888888888888888888888888888888888888888
Copyright Acknowledgements:
Janis Astor del Valle, I'LL BE HOME PARA LA NAVIDAD (c) 1993, WHERE THE SEÑORITAS ARE
(c) 1993, poems MAMI'S BALLET (c) 1991, AFRICAN SEEDS (c) 1992;
Pamela S. Simones, SINS OF THE MOTHERS (c) 1991;
Anne M. Harris, COMING IN;
Cheryl J. Moore, SIS TUCKER; WOMAN THE CENTER;
Lynn Emidia, THE REVELATION GAME; EBONY LOVE;
Pam Cady, THE SECRET LIFE OF PLANTS;
Caitlin Cain, THRU THESE EYES EACH OTHER A LOOKING GLASS;
Ira L. Jeffries, CLOTEL (c) 1990 and MANCHILD (c) 1992.

Womyn
of the
Moon

Acknowledgement to original photographers and artists Ana R. Kissed (lesbian images from
ana.r.kissed and 1989 Wombyn's Calendar), Cindy Hardin and Lee Bowers, Myriam Fougère, April
A.Torres, Lisa M. Wright (Imagine Images), Monique Frugier (Monar Cards), Ellen Symons, Dawn
Manna, Jacque Harper and Ruth Brose; Phyllis RoseChild and Sharon - photos of their handiwork.
88888888888888888888888888888888888888888888888888888888888888888888

The Editor wishes to express gratitude to the talented PLAYWRIGHTS,
ARTISTS and POETS whose perception and creativity comprise this
volume, and to all the womyn who submitted plays.  A special heartfelt
thanks to playwright Pam Simones who suggested the title, TORCH TO
THE HEART (from Sappho), then later wrote the brilliant introduction; to
photographer/writer Ana R. Kissed who searched through her albums while
recovering from a winter cold (sent over 30 inspirational photos); to Karen
Campbell for her proofreading expertise; to Lynn P, whose gentle concern
led me from the *possible* to the *real;* to Dee M, Betty S, Cathy B, and Jolene
M for their encouragement; to the Women Playwrights Collective and
writers Carolyn Gage and Rosemary Curb (wishing them success with their
upcoming projects) for their imput during our brief encounters; to founder of
LACE Productions, Patty Gwozdz a timely review; to Cynthia for her atten-
tions; to my children and family members for their uncompromising love.

# TORCH TO THE HEART
## ANTHOLOGY OF LESBIAN ART AND DRAMA

*Edited by Sue McConnell-Celi, M.A.*

*With a Special Introduction by*
*PAMELA SIMONES*

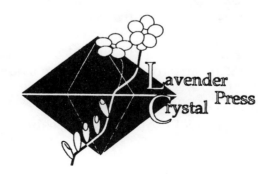

**LAVENDER CRYSTAL PRESS**
**NEW JERSEY**

LAVENDER CRYSTAL PRESS
PO Box 8932
Red Bank, NJ 07701

TORCH TO THE HEART Anthology of Lesbian Art and Drama

ISBN  1-884541-00-3
Printed in the U.S.A.

**Sue McConnell-Celi,** received a B.S. from Seton Hall University with a major in English Education in the '60's, having been one of the first women to attend the Seton Hall Campus. Ten years later, while raising four children and holding down two jobs, she earned an M.A. in Reading Specialization from Kean College, eventually teaching grades 7 through college for many years. This fifty-two year old grandmother of six has been an active human rights proponent since that time, beginning with the Daughters of Bilitis (NYC chapter), the first lesbian organization in America. In the early days of N.O.W, she lobbied in Trenton for women's rights - equal pay for equal work - and for lesbian and gay rights, meeting with legislators on several occasions. In the '70's, she founded the Lesbian Mother's Union and the first N.J. based Gay Activist Alliance in Essex County, holding memberships in Leagaue of Women Voters then, and in 1990 (writer/Board member). As a former journalist (1980-1990), her weekly column, "Woman About Town" (local newspaper) covered political events and human interest stories; she was forever grateful to have had the opportunity to develop her writing skills while meeting wonderful people. She held board memberships in two civic groups. In 1990, her attentions turned to radio, producing/hosting a variety of lesbian and gay radio shows for New Jersey (On the Line) and New York/ Connecticut/NJ based Radio Pacifica (WBAI), meeting some of the most dynamic individuals in the lesbigay community. (One lively show examined LESBIANS AND GAYS IN THE ARTS. Artist Myriam Fougere was among the invited). A published poet in a monthly magazine, THE NETWORK and COMMON LIVES, LESBIAN LIVES, she began writing reviews of lesbian written/focused books which have appeared in SAPPHO'S ISLE, N.Y.; THE NETWORK, New Jersey's Lesbian and Gay Magazine, LAVENDER EXPRESS and publications throughout the nation highlighting authors such as Karla Jay and Joanne Glasgow (*LESBIAN TEXTS AND CONTEXTS; Radical Revisions*, NYU Press 1990), Anita Pace *(WRITE FROM THE HEART, Lesbians Healing From Heartache,* Baby Steps Press, 1992), and Virginia Mollenkott *(SENSUOUS SPIRITUALITY, Out From Fundamentalism,* Crossroads Press, 1992). She has co/facilitated myriad workshops including SISTERSPACE, Pennsylvania, NJEA, Atlantic City Convention, GAAMC, and local schools and colleges. A 1991 recipient of the New Jersey Lesbian and Gay Coalition Annual Achievement Award, she had the distinguished honor of being the first Lesbian Human Relations Commissioner in her state, 1990-92, along with dozens of community, religious, legal and educational leaders, to help forge a new future of equality for ALL people. In 1993, while recovering from major surgery, she took out a pension loan to self-publish her first book, a collection of essays, narratives, poems, photos, cartoons and curricula by teachers and students -- *TWENTY-FIRST CENTURY CHALLENGE: LESBIANS AND GAYS IN EDUCATION-BRIDGING THE GAP.* Thus, the beginning of **LAVENDER CRYSTAL PRESS.**

# Foreword

Drama and the arts, a prism to the people it serves. At its best, it represents the widest possible spectrum of that society, both witnessing and reflecting its dreams as well as its realities. The Works contained within this volume introduce emerging lesbian artists and dramatists, expressing the rich imagery and symbolism inherent in our culture. On the threshold of a new era, with courage and vision, lesbians are now approaching the public media through film (such as popular movies, DESERT HEARTS/CLAIRE OF THE MOON), theatre and the arts - a movement perhaps captured by the gaze of the "Dyke in the Doorway" (cover photo by photographer/artist/writer Ana R. Kissed).

My first exposure to lesbian drama was Off Broadway, near Sheridan Square - LAST SUMMER AT BLUEFISH COVE by Jane Chambers. The tiny theatre was packed. During the intermission, the audience - womyn from all parts of the tri-state area - shared their excitement and views of this excellent play - a brilliant production depicting a small group of friends who get together one summer to reminisce old times with the main character (who has only a short time to live). I felt lucky to have caught the play just a few performances before it closed. It was years to come before I would find myself, again, in the seat of a packed-to-capacity theater, only this time it was the third-floor room of the NYC Lesbian and Gay Community Service Center. I especially recall one vibrant play - though they were all memorable - a Janis Astor del Valle comedy. *A lesbian comedy!* The plot revolved around a womyn who takes her best (straight) friend, whom she believes is not lesbophobic, to a lesbian beach at Cherry Grove, *for the first time!* (WHERE THE SEÑORITAS ARE - an excerpt of the full length play is included in this volume). A departure from the serious plots I knew, it was also witty and insightful. (Have we come that far? I thought).

In the last decade, numerous plays with lesbian centered themes have been written *and produced*, hence making available a vast pool of talent

During the summer of '93, I was asked to publish a book of lesbian drama. After thinking about it for all of five seconds, I agreed. While preparing press releases, I decided that the visual, too, was important - frequently, pictures draw readers into literature. Images of wonderful artwork - sculpture, ceramics, paintings, photography - I had seen at the annual EAST COAST LESBIAN FESTIVAL popped into my mind - womyn-centered, reflective, real. I was proud of our artistic legacy and found it healing and self-empowering (especially the nudes portrayed by lesbians - decidedly not the usual "come-get-me" variety). So, the word *ART* was added to announcements. By November, 31 plays had arrived; by mid-December, 60 photos, 15 poems.

All artists are included in TORCH TO THE HEART; however, due to (very) limited finances and space, nine plays were selected, seven playwrights in all. Representing a diversity of age, race, ethnicity and (political/philosophical) viewpoint, these evocative scripts revolve around issues of concern to us all - racism, rape, incest survival (Lynn Emidia's, THE REVELATION GAME and Caitlin Cain's THRU THESE GLASSES WE'VE SEEN OURSELVES EACH OTHER A LOOKING GLASS deal with the latter two), love recaptured, coming out (to mother, to grandmother, to father) *and* COMING IN (a satire by Anne Harris, founder of LEND International, in which lesbian moms are shocked that their daughter is dating a boy:   "She hasn't even touched the Birkenstocks we bought...")  And speaking of those favorite leather sandals, we get a first-hand view of lesbian culture in each of these plays, not to mention, lesbian wisdom (Pamela Simones' characters discuss oral tradition and the wisdom of older womyn, "...Everywoman should have a croning party.")  You can learn a lot from a lesbian - her observations, her self-reliant strength, her ability to survive/transcend oppression.  It is also inevitable that part of our herstory, the dyke bar rituals, would be included (CLOTEL, a character piece by Ira L. Jeffries), as well as the complicated topic, dating, which one romantic comedy flirts with (Pam Cady, THE SECRET LIFE OF PLANTS) while two lovers try to define their relationship.

I hope the drama and artwork in this anthology provide an entertaining glimpse into our lives, create greater understanding and self-empowerment, and bring us closer to the vision and promise beheld by the "Dyke in the Doorway".

> - Sue McConnell-Celi, Editor
> January, 1994

*"Meredith Playing Pool" from IMAGINE IMAGES by Lisa M. Wright*

# CONTENTS

Foreword **vi**

WOMEN AND THEATER: A SHORT OVERVIEW,
Introduction by Pamela S. Simones **xiv**

## PLAYS ~

ix

# POEMS ~

# ARTWORK / PHOTOS ~

# BIOGRAPHIES

*Information about Myriam Fougère,*
*Monique Frugier, Dawn D. Manna,*
*Jacque Harper and Ruth Brose*

# WOMEN AND THEATRE:
## A SHORT OVERVIEW
### Introduction by Pamela S. Simones

Hrotsvith von Gandersheim (935-973) was a German nun who wrote liturgical plays in exquisite Latin. A woman in a community of women, she was writing at a time when Saxon kings still ruled England. In the 70's, one university press published a translation of Hrotsvith's plays. There is nothing to indicate Hrotsvith was a lesbian. The important thing to remember is the community of women who supported her.

*MOROCCAN DOOR*  **photo by Monique Frugier**

*"Read, see, listen, experience women creating and create yourself. Carry the torch to the heart of things. Light up the places which have been kept secret."*

*- Pamela S. Simones*

Theater is not a solitary act. It presumes an audience. I define theatre as the use of language and body movement to evoke a recognition or response in the audience. Obviously, early rituals are theatre by this definition. As matrifocal belief systems were overthrown by patriarchal ones, women were relegated to less than equal status and were banned from the temple as well as from the centers of education and the arts. Theatre became an exclusive male province. Women were not encouraged to speak, particularly not in public, most definitely not on a raised platform in front of an audience.

But some women were compelled to fly in the face of authority. Although the Church was a prime mover against the freedom of women, at least two other nuns made names for themselves as playwrights - Suor Annalena Odaldi (1572-1638) in Italy and Sor Juana (1651-1695) in Mexico.

A benchmark for all women is the arrival of Aphra Behn (1640-1689). She is hailed as the first woman to earn her living by the pen and was second only to Dryden in popularity and production during her lifetime. She was a merry widow who deplored marriage and enjoyed the favors of both men and women but did not live to see her reputation used as an excuse to nearly obliterate her accomplishments. Susanna Centlivre (1669-1723) dressed as a boy in order to study at Cambridge. She issued her plays under an assumed name in order to avoid calumny. Delarivier Manley so embodied the licentious aspect of a woman in the arts that her talent has all but been totally unacknowledged. Mrs. Inchbald (1753-1821) avoided censure by becoming known more as a novelist and less as a playwright. In fact, many women who started as playwrights turned to other venues, most notably Americans Susan Glaspell and Lillian Hellman.

In her 1914 work, **The Social Significance of the Modern Drama,** Emma Goldman would write, "Both the radical and the conservative have to learn that any mode of creative work, which with true perception portrays social wrongs earnestly and boldly, may be a greater menace to our social fabric and a more powerful inspiration than the wildest harangue of the soapbox orator."

Conventional theatre was so anti-female, traditional, and conservative - and still is - that many women and minorities chose to start their own theatre groups. In England, suffragists formed their own theatre. In America, the Provincetown Players, Washington Square Playhouse, Harlem Experimental Theatre and Krigwa Players gave women and African Americans a chance to be produced.

Notable lesbian authors also wrote for the stage: Gertrude Stein, Edna St. Vincent Millay, Djuna Barnes, and Natalie Barney. Theatre at last was recognized as a way to address social issues. There are now many women's theatre groups which use drama as a means to raise political consciousness.

As long as theatre is defined as a small area of real estate in New York City, there will be scant room for women and women's causes on the stage. But if we work together to create, speak, act up, theatre will become a vibrant living medium. If you would like to do something political, read plays by Jane Chambers, Claudia Allen, Judy Grahn. Form a theatre group. Recover "lost" women writers. Support women's theatre groups. Read, see, listen, experience women creating and create yourself. Carry the torch to the heart of things. Light up the places which have been kept secret.

**Pamela Sue Simones, librarian, playwright in residence for a local Theatre Company, creates scripts that deal with women's issues.**

# TORCH TO THE HEART
## Anthology of Lesbian Art and Drama

*"FOR LESBIAN EYES"*
*Sculpture: Myriam Fougère*

# WOMAN, THE CENTER
## by Cheryl J. Moore

She is in a silence
   that marks her spirit.
Today she lets the rain
   keep her
      as her thoughts look for the moon.
   She brings stones and bridges ~
      she brings paper.
Clouds are words
    and she reads
the holy spring, the green sea.
Her rain reflects her
talking eye, and a poem
   is an apple on the table.

*Sunday Morning    Photography by Ana R. Kissed*

# SIS JANE TUCKER
## by Cheryl J. Moore

My mother's mother, Janie Eugenia Paulk, seldom spoke~
She didn't chat.  She tempered her actions and

I can't tell how she sailed so serious.  She saw nothing
To joke about when she sat rocking with her eyes closed

Of an evening.
She was a seamstress with straight pins in a breast of

Her sometime vest.  She sewed green cotton covering
The rocking chair near a fireplace, sewed dresses

For the white ladies on Peach Street.
Their big houses were of kitchen furniture and oddments~

Light curtains, forbidden living room.  Grandma
Prayed standing up.  I thought it was prayer.

But a distance lay in her face of a past, a love.
Gentle face, but one looked rather at her presence.

She meditated.  In evening I combed her hair that she
Kept knotted in a bun.  She showed me what to do

By her timing and the flicker of her bent hands that beat
A waltz in her heart, her one liveliness.

Oh, but she could erupt of a day, and she meant it,
To adult or child.

*Her matriarch head was a silent law to men and women.*
*She bore herself with gravity, perhaps learned in*

*Africa. She said sweetbread.*
*Her time was the reckoning black*

*Nineteenth century in the early half of the white twentieth.*
*She brought African prose to Ocilla and some way of walking.*

*Standing in her century. The close of her archaic words*
*Stood me still with their love, some year.*

*Imagine her missionary work, living in a tribal hut*
*On dirt floors, careful of snakes, a python,*

*Teaching the black African talking women to sew samplers.*
*Grandma returned what she found, Africa, without a why.*

◆◆◆◆◆◆◆◆◆◆◆◆◆◆◆◆◆◆◆◆◆◆◆◆◆◆◆◆◆◆◆◆◆◆◆◆◆◆◆◆◆

**CHERYL J. MOORE,
Asbury Park, New
Jersey was born
in Georgia, 1947.
She began writing
in 1980. Her poems
are from a
manuscript called,
"Paper and Colors".
One of her
short stories
was published in
SINISTER WISDOM, #49.**

**CHERYL J. MOORE**

5

**Photo by Ana R. Kissed**

*"You didn't do anything, Dee.  It's me.  I'm the problem.
I don't know how to say this.   It's so hard..."*
*~ THE REVELATION GAME*

# THE REVELATION GAME
## by Lynn Emidia

### CHARACTERS

SYLVIE: *Born and bred New Yorker, 35ish, hip, sophistocated, intelligent, good sense of humor but troubled.*

DEE: *Lives in Jersey, 45 or so, also quite hip, sophistocated and intelligent but not too easily reached.*

ROSALIND: *Therapist, 50ish, dresses impeccably, very confident. She is Sylvie's 'sounding board'.*

*Summer, 1992.*
*A quiet restaurant somewhere in lower Manhattan.*

### SCENE ONE

SYLVIE *(At a table for two seated across from Dee)* I think I'm feeling a little scared of you.

DEE Really? I thought my questions piqued your curiosity. You appear to be somewhat intrigued by them.

SYLVIE Not as much as my fear of the intensity I feel coming from you.

DEE It's just frenetic energy I release.

SYLVIE I don't know what to do with it.

7

DEE *(Leans into her)* Don't do anything with it, just use it to energize yourself.

SYLVIE But I find myself inhaling so deeply I'm almost at a point of hyperventilation.

DEE Then you better start carrying paper bags to breathe into.

SYLVIE *(Laughs)* That's what I like about you Dee, you find just the right moment to throw in a zinger.

DEE Yeah, zing go the strings...So, what'll it be Sylvie, baby? A night on the town or do we just sit here topping each other with scintillating conversation?

SYLVIE Conversation seems to be your forte. You really have an uncanny capability for setting a mood. I'm perfectly happy to stay right here.

DEE OK then...how shall we play the game?

SYLVIE Game? I don't think I understand.

DEE You don't have to understand...you just have to listen very closely...and react...here's your first question. *(Tone changes)* What criteria would you set for that 'perfect' person?

SYLVIE Don't beat around the bush, Dee. Can't you ask a more direct question?

DEE Come on, I'm serious. *(A little angry)* You wanted to play, so don't make up your own rules!

SYLVIE How can I make up rules if I don't even know what

the game is?

DEE   Look, we don't have to stay here.  We can leave and do what other mundane couples do and go clubbing if that's what you want.

SYLVIE   No.  No, Dee...I want to play...it's just that I'm a little uneasy about what it is that you want from me.

DEE   *(Angrier)*   I just want you to answer the damn question!

SYLVIE   OK!  Fine!  You'll have to repeat it.  I've lost my train of thought a little.

DEE   One of the main rules, if you want rules, is never lose your train of thought because that's one sure fire way of losing points...OK I'm only repeating this because you're a novice player...What would be the one thing you would need to make that difference in choosing that perfect someone?

SYLVIE   *(Pauses taking a deep breath)*   Sharing one infinitesimal moment of perfect fusion that suspends you in time.

DEE   That's rather poetic.  Do you write?

SYLVIE   A little.

DEE   Well, you should do it more.

SYLVIE   I need tangible inspiration.

DEE   *(Rises)*  See, here I am.   (Holds out her hands and spins around.)  Use me.

SYLVIE   You mean now?

DEE   *(Playful)*   Why not?  If you need a surge of energy to ignite your creativity, I'm yours.

SYLVIE   I'm embarrassed.

DEE   Come on, come on...do it...*(sits and leans into her.)*   say it to me...tell me your poetic fantasies out loud...the dreams you relate on paper...come on...

SYLVIE   *(Now caught up in her excitement.)*   You want subtle reality or nebulous imaginings?

DEE   *(Leaning back in her chair, arms folded.)*   Whatever turns you on.

SYLVIE   OK...let me see if I can remember what I entered in my journal last night...Velvet trade winds transcend the stealth of night   *(stops)*   Dee, I really feel self-conscious   *(looks around.)*

DEE   Look, nobody's aware we're even here...now, close your eyes and breathe in deeply...go with it...come on...*(whispering)* come on...

SYLVIE   *(Takes a deep breath)*   Velvet trade winds transcend. Cobalt waves slap against the hull...lulling us as we repose...briefly.   *(Opens her eyes and stares at her.)*   Well? What?

DEE   *(Rises, crosses behind her and whispers in her ear.)*   I think I just got turned on...

*(Lights Fade.)*

## SCENE TWO

*One month later. Psychotherapist's office somewhere on the upper West Side of Manhattan.*

SYLVIE   (*Enter, pacing, talking*)   Hi, hi...

ROSALIND   (*Seated with pad and pencil.*)   Don't you want to sit, Sylvie?

SYLVIE   No, not yet.  I'm too hyper...(*continues pacing*).

ROSALIND   Are you having trouble sleeping again?

SYLVIE   Only once this week   (*leans against the window sill*).

ROSALIND   You've been having those nightmares again?

SYLVIE   Hoo boy, have I!  This one was slightly more violent than the others.

ROSALIND   Well, you were really going through a period of depression last year that would certainly account for those bad dreams.  So what now?

SYLVIE   I honestly don't know what in hell prompted this one but you can see I have this really bad fear, phobia or whatever you want to call it...of axes...you know...hatchets.  Well, this dream was really mixed up with my ex-mother-in-law and my husband...and me wanting to shut them up.  And then suddenly for no apparent reason I'm whacking and hacking my way through my kitchen...the next thing I know, I'm sitting straight

*11*

up in my bed, nightclothes soaked through and heaving so hard I can't catch my breath!

ROSALIND   (*She's been sitting on the edge of her seat and now leans back.*)   Actually, it appears to be a dream purely for release of tension.  These nightmarish type dreams can be beneficial in reducing stress.  Feel better now?  (*Sylvie nods.*) So, how was the rest of your week?

SYLVIE   You know, now I'm really confused.  Dee and I spent this past Saturday doing nice things for each other for a change. I bought her a kite that we flew together in Central Park and then she took me on a ride up the Hudson.  Ya know, I've lived in New York all my life and never been on that boat!

ROSALIND   Yes, I know what you mean.  I've never been to the top of the Empire State Building.  OK so...what happened? Sounds like it was a good week aside from your night sweats with Lizzy Borden and company.

SYLVIE   Well, it was good...to a point.  Our conversation was back to what it was when we first met.  Remember?

ROSALIND   Yes, that lesbian singles bar in the Village...uh what's its name?

SYLVIE   Singles my ass!  How come a person can only see you on Saturdays...in the daytime and not at night and...never on a Sunday.  Sounds like the song, huh?  Who the hell knew she had a doctor husband, two kids and a fifteen room bungalow in Jersey?

ROSALIND   Didn't you tell me she had an apartment in the city?

SYLVIE   Oh, you mean the passion pit up on 72nd?  Humph!
It is impressive though...right down to the mirrored ceiling and
black satin sheets.  Did you ever fuck on satin sheets?  It's all
true.  You find yourself sliding right the hell outta the damned
bed and watching yourself as you go!  (*They laugh.*)

ROSALIND   Come on Sylvie, let's discuss your conversation -
does it sound like where it had been when you two first met?

SYLVIE   Yeah, yeah...it was that playful kind of bantering back
and forth.  You know, playing the dozens, one upman but with a
clever twist to it.

ROSALIND   But you time together lately has been very tense.
What do you think caused this turnabout?

SYLVIE   I honestly don't know but then Dee's moods seem to
change with the wind.  So, who's to say when she chose to play
again.

(*Lights fade on Rosalind, come up on Dee who's seated next to
Sylvie.*)

DEE   I liked the kite, Sylvie, but you know, you didn't have to.

SYLVIE   Why not?  You need to fly a kite.  It expands and
frees your soul.

DEE   My soul?  How do you know what my soul needs?

SYLVIE   I know you were smiling the whole time the thing
was up in the air...except when it took a nosedive on that jogger
in the park.  (*They both laugh.*)  I like to hear you laugh...You
do it so rarely.

*13*

DEE   Well, I haven't got a whole hell of a lot in my life to laugh at. (*Pause.*)   Sylvie, what do you least like about me?

SYLVIE   What do I least like about you?   That's a stupid question.   It's too hard.   Ask me something else.

DEE   No.   I mean it.   Answer me.

SYLVIE   Why do you constantly play these mind games with me?

DEE   Because you like it.   You're quick, you're smart.

SYLVIE   I can't think as fast as you think I can.   And besides, what kind of answer do you want?

DEE   That 's just it Sylvie, I don't want pat answers.   I want you to think, use that terrific mind of yours and play off me.

SYLVIE   Play off you!   What the hell does that mean?

DEE   Look why can't you just answer my question?   (*Getting louder and annoyed.*)

SYLVIE   I already forgot what you asked.   You get me nuts! Sometimes I just can't keep up with you.

DEE   OK then...let's change the question. (*Pauses to think*) ...why do you find the sea so compelling?

*The Beach at Atlantic City*
*Photo by Sue McConnell-Celi*

14

SYLVIE   Dee, you know how I feel about the sea.   It's exciting!  It generates my energy and ignites my spirit!

DEE   (*Leans into Sylvie getting caught up in her words...She's actually getting off on what Sylvie says.*)   That's it...that's it...keep it up...

SYLVIE   (*She stands and looks away from her breathing heavily.*)   The surge of the ebb and the flow...all consuming. The smell of the kelp and driftwood drying in the sun   (*leans on the back of the chair with both arms)*...the wind rushing through my hair whipping it over my face and shoulders...

DEE   (*Rises, crosses and comes up behind her.  Sylvie straightens up, she puts her lips to Sylvie's ear)*...as I lean into you, chest to back, (*her hands are not touching Sylvie but around her holding on to the back of the chair, trapping her)*...breathing my breath into your soul, inhaling your essence, whispering I want you...(*now puts her arms around her).*

SYLVIE   (*Breaks away.*)   Don't do that!

DEE   (*Angrily grabs her by the arm.*)   Listen Sylvie, don't push me away like that!

SYLVIE   (*Snaps back.*)   Then don't come up on me like that!

DEE   (*Changing her tone.*)   Come on baby (*cross sits*) you know you love this game.

SYLVIE   That's just it Dee, it IS a game and it's great...so let's keep it in perspective.  The fantasy is how we get off here! (*Angrily*)  Alright!  OK!  You really want to know what I least like about you?  (Pause)  It's your temper.  (*She gets really*

*15*

*quiet.*) It...scares me.

DEE   Scares you?  No, no, no, uh, uh, I don't buy
that...Frankly, I think my volatility (*lowers voice*) excites you...
(*Lights fade on Sylvie, up on Rosalind.*)

ROSALIND   Well, Sylvie does it?  ARE you titillated by her
outbursts?

SYLVIE   Are you serious?  Her fits of anger scare the shit out
of me.  It's like deja vu.  I'm suddenly transported back in time
to my fuckin' marriage and I want to vomit.

ROSALIND   That's a pretty violent reaction.  Does Dee remind
you of your ex-husband?

SYLVIE   Not a whole lot...but this mind game playing and the
sudden attacks...there is some parallel...something that sends a
shudder through my bones...You know, it's the unpredictability
that I find so exciting, not the volatility.  Dee thrives on probing
and confrontation.  She really gets off on challenging me and I
feed right into her...(*searching for the right words*)...creative
explorations of my inner consciousness.

ROSALIND   But Sylvie, you do seem to get a sense of
excitement when Dee does this fantasy thing with you.

SYLVIE   Fantasies ARE exciting because they spark and tempt
you into a safe...but unreal world...and Dee does that well.  She's
very creative.

ROSALIND   So are you.

SYLVIE   Yes, we're a good match in that department.

*16*

ROSALIND   Why do you suppose you do that...feed her I mean.  Does being preyed upon give you some kind of feeling of "poor little me I'm so vulnerable and I can only feel needed if I let this person walk all over me"?

SYLVIE   Damn it Ros, why the hell do I do this to myself?  Intellectually I know that this kind of relationship is gnawing my guts out but yet I fall for the same kind of person that just eats holes in my brain and sucks out my soul...(*she wells up and tears are apparent.*)

ROSALIND   Sylvie, Sylvie I know this is hard but that's why you're here and don't worry, we'll do this together.  I'm here for you.  Let's try to go on.  You still have ten minutes (*glances at watch*).  Did she have any more of her probing questions?

SYLVIE   You better believe it.  It did not end there.
*(Lights fade on Rosalind and come up on Dee.)*

DEE   *(She's standing behind a chair looking out away from Sylvie)*   Sylvie, how would you feel if someone started to cry when you first made love?

SYLVIE   Damn it, do we have to talk about this? (*Rises, paces*).

DEE   I'm asking you a reasonable question under the circumstances.  Now, answer me! (*voice grows louder, she spins Sylvie around forcing her to face her.*)  How would you feel?

SYLVIE   (*Almost inaudibly*)...I would feel I had done something wrong.

DEE   What?  What did you say?

*17*

SYLVIE  (*Yells now*)  I would feel I had done something wrong!

DEE   See what I mean?  Look at the answer you just gave me!
What do you think was going through my mind that first time
and each time thereafter.  You, you just switched off at tone
point.  I don't understand...Are you going to tell me what
happened or what?  What did I do?

SYLVIE   You didn't do anything, Dee.  It's me.  I'm the
problem.  I don't know how to say this.  It's so hard...(*she
returns to her seat.  Dee follows and sits too*)  Dee, I was having
a flashback...it was the sex, not you.  You're a wonderful
lover...it's just that...oh God, this is so hard...the feeling is so
overwhelming...it feels like I suddenly can't breathe and I just
want to be somewhere else and then...I started to cry.  I felt so
totally out of control...

DEE   I don't understand.  I still had to have done something to
set you off!

SYLVIE   Gees, Dee, I'm telling you it wasn't YOU!  It was the
sex.  It could have been ANYONE.  It was the sex...it triggered
my thoughts and I just couldn't relax enough for you to get me
to come!

(*Lights fade on Dee and come up on Rosalind.*)

...As a matter of fact, I never let anyone do that to me anyway...

ROSALIND   Do what?

SYLVIE   Get me to come!  I was always in control no matter
who the person was.  No one was ever going to do that to me
again!  (*She's really agitated*).

ROSALIND   OK, Sylvie, calm down.  I need to know what you meant.  Let's go back a little to when you mentioned having flashbacks.  What was it you were seeing?

SYLVIE   (*She pauses and obviously has a difficult time answering.*)   Oh God...Ros, I saw my rape...and I was not even twelve...

(*Lights fade to blackout.*)


## SCENE THREE

*Fall.  Park bench somewhere in Central Park.*

DEE   (*They both are seated.*)   I can't believe you didn't tell me right away!

SYLVIE   Oh sure...(*shakes Dee's hand.*)   How do you do.  My name is Sylvie and I was raped when I was a little girl...and what's your story?   (*Let's go of her hand.*)

DEE   Come on Sylvie, don't joke around.   This is serious.

SYLVIE   You bet your ass it is.

DEE   I'm really nervous about this.  What if I can't handle this?

SYLVIE   What are you saying here Dee?

DEE   Well, I mean I've never had an experience like this.

SYLVIE   Oh, and I have.

*19*

DEE   For heaven's sake, help me out here.

SYLVIE   Help YOU out!  I'm the one seeing the shrink!

DEE   Don't hide behind your doctor's pad and pencil, Sylvie.

SYLVIE   And what is that supposed to mean?

DEE   I mean let's talk about this.  Can't you tell me how it happened?

SYLVIE   Is this one of your fantasy games Dee, or what?

DEE   I just want to understand.

SYLVIE   Is this to help you or me?

DEE   To help each other.

SYLVIE   OK, so we help each other.  I get better, you get fucked and then what?

DEE   What the hell are you leading up to here Sylvie?

SYLVIE   I mean just that...then what?  Do we live happily ever after?  Is that the ultimate fantasy...the fairy tale ending to our GAME?  Or, is the reality of this all going to finally hit the fan?

DEE   Just what is it that you expect of me?

SYLVIE   Damn it Dee, can't you say the words?

DEE   You mean, I have a husband, two kids and a house in the suburbs?

SYLVIE   *(She starts to laugh and Dee joins her.)*   How do you like that?

DEE   What?

SYLVIE   Twist things around so I forget to be mad.

DEE   So, do I have to wait for you to get in the mood or what?

SYLVIE   *(Still playful)*   What...

DEE   *(She sobers)*   Stop it Sylvie!

SYLVIE   *(Snaps back angrily)*   Why?  So you can probe me for all the answers to your stupid questions.

DEE   Stupid?  I don't think my asking you about this rape is stupid.  If we're going to continue with this relationship don't you think I have the right to some answers?

SYLVIE   Right?  Right?  You can't be serious.  You have no right because you can't commit!  You have a husband!  It's plain as hell!

DEE   I don't think we need to continue with this conversation.  You're not playing fair.

SYLVIE   Ah ha!  So, this IS another game!

DEE   Fuck you, Sylvie!

(Lights fade on Dee and come up on Rosalind.)

ROSALIND   So, she doesn't like the rules.  So, she picks up her bat and ball and goes home.

SYLVIE   Yeah, to the little hubby and kiddies in Jersey.

ROSALIND   Alright, enough about Dee for the moment.  Did you work on trying to write about your rape?

SYLVIE   Ros, this was the hardest task I've ever undertaken.  I had a hard time starting out but I remembered what you said about trying to relax before beginning.  So, I took a cordial glass of brandy, a pad and pencil, curled up on my sofa with my mother's afghan that she knitted and sipped until I was really feeling mellow.  *(Pause)*   I pictured myself and how I felt when I was eleven...my friends, my neighborhood, my house, my street...the time of year.  It really started to flood into my mind...*(closes her eyes)*...the smells...my sweater, my Keds, my blue jeans...and Howard, my boyfriend.  *(Pause, opens her eyes)*  How could he betray me like that?  *(Getting louder)*  How could he let them do that to me?  *(Starts to dry heave)*  It made me sick to my stomach.  I wanted to vomit.  I couldn't yell  *(louder yet)*   because someone was holding my mouth and I couldn't breathe...because I was...*(softer)*   so scared  *(starts to weep)*.

ROSALIND   Sylvie, Sylvie it's OK.  Just let it out, you're doing great.  Can you go on?  Who was there besides Howard?

SYLVIE   His two buddies, Marty and another boy...I can't remember his name.  We went into the woods near my house just to make out...Howard and me...*(blows her nose)*   Marty and the other kid were supposed to be our lookouts...you know, to warn us if someone was coming.  I remember Howard finding a big cardboard box and he and the guys ripping it apart so they could lay it on the damp ground cause it was only spring...and there was an odor...of rusty earth mixed with wet cardboard that

I have not forgotten to this moment. There was a smell about Howard and Marty too. Boy smell...and sex smell...*(starts to heave again)*.

ROSALIND   It's OK...You're safe here...Just try to go on.

SYLVIE   *(Takes a deep breath)*   That's the point thing start to get fuzzy. I don't actually remember the whole thing clearly. It's kind of disjointed.

ROSALIND   Well, at least try to talk of what you do remember.

SYLVIE   Marty came over at one point and told Howard to stop because it was his turn. I didn't know what he meant. I didn't understand. What did he mean? *(At this point she is almost in a trance; gets louder.)*   Marty is all over me...he's on top of me...I can't breathe! What's he doing? Why are you doing this! Someone is lying behind me...breathing heavy down my neck and in my ear...I'm surrounded...enveloped...choking! Oh, God, *(shouts)* LET ME GO!   *(She lurches forward.)*

ROSALIND   Sylvie, it's OK, it's OK   *(grabs her hand)* Hold on to me. You're safe here. You're OK...can you go on?

SYLVIE   Why did they do that? I was only a kid and they were 15. How did they think they would get away with it?

ROSALIND   Did they?

SYLVIE   Yes...

ROSALIND   How? Didn't you tell anyone? Your mother? *(Lets her hand go so she can continue writing.)*

*23*

SYLVIE No, I couldn't. I was the good little girl who followed directions. This was a violation of the rules. I WILLINGLY went into the woods with a boy to LET him touch me.

ROSALIND But you had no idea what was about to happen.

SYLVIE (*Shouts*) That son of a bitch, Howard! How could he betray me like that? That fucking son of a bitch! They said if I told, that they would tell everybody that I was a slut, a whore and that I wanted it! (*Quieter*)...and I believed them...

ROSALIND So you told no one?

SYLVIE No one...Not 'til today...25 years later.

ROSALIND (*Pause*) Well, my dear, you've taken some big steps. What you've done here today was the best thing that could have happened. You let go of a secret that you've harbored all too long...by yourself.

SYLVIE Now what?

ROSALIND You go on.

SYLVIE Go on?

ROSALIND Of course. We'll work together for there is a healing process to experience. It's almost like the twelve steps you take as a recovering alcoholic or co-dependent. There's a lot for you to work on.

SYLVIE And Dee?

ROSALIND What about her?

SYLVIE   Exactly.  What about her?

ROSALIND   Well, Sylvie, looks like you have a decision to
make here.  Do you care enough about her to mount all these
obstacles or do you walk away?  Only you know the answer to
this one.

SYLVIE   Right.  She's obsessive, compulsive, volatile,
exciting...married...but I know she cares.

ROSALIND   What makes you believe that?

SYLVIE   Because she didn't walk away.  Ya know, she's great
looking.  She's got plenty of money, a super career...she could
have any woman she wants without all the complications I've
brought into  his relationship.  But she DIDN'T WALK AWAY.
She chose to try to understand and talk about it.

ROSALIND   Could the reason be that this is just another
challenge for her?  You said she likes that.

SYLVIE   Oh, come on Ros, this is a little different and goes far
beyond an intoxicating fantasy.  She revels in game-playing but
this is jolting reality and don't you see for the first time in this
relationship the game is not important.  I am.

ROSALIND   OK Sylvie.  Sounds like you may have good
direction but it's not the Yellow Brick Road to Emerald City.

*(Lights fade to blackout.)*


**SCENE FOUR**

*Two weeks later. Same restaurant as the first scene.*

SYLVIE   Well, how are you?

DEE   How should I be?

SYLVIE   Look Dee, we haven't seen each other in two weeks, there should be a lot to talk about.

DEE   Oh really, so you can listen with only half an ear?

SYLVIE   What the hell are you talking about?

DEE   Listen Sylvie, I don't like it when you seem to fade away in the middle of my conversations with you.

SYLVIE   I'm sorry, but I'm completely unaware that I do that and I don't do it on purpose.

DEE   Don't patronize me Sylvie, you sound like you're spewing lines from a well-rehearsed script!

SYLVIE   I don't want to fight with you.  I didn't come here to confront you in battle.

DEE   Then why do you do that?  You get this look of vagueness and you look right through me.

SYLVIE   Don't make me the victim here Dee!  Maybe I'm just a little tired of listening to your ramblings.  Your bemoaning of your unsatisfactory life, how you hate your job, your husband and how you can't cope with getting older.

DEE   If you don't like what I say then why do you stay?

SYLVIE   Because I thought I loved you.

DEE   Thought?  Are we speaking in past tense?

SYLVIE   It does appear that way.  Dee, this relationship or
whatever you want to call it has never really taken shape.  We
talk...on the phone...we see each other only when it's convenient
for you...when you can slip away, when you don't have to be
with the family...when you don't have to work.  I'm only an
appointment in your schedule of the day.  (*Pretends to leaf
through a book.*)   Let's see here now, staff meeting at nine
AM...lunch with Sylvie at noon...back to the office at two.

DEE   You didn't complain before.  It was exciting for you.

SYLVIE   That's because I didn't care at that point.  It was
exciting...the secrecy of it all.  But it went too far.  I fell in love
with you.

DEE   How can you say that when we couldn't even have a
normal sexual relationship!

SYLVIE   If you really cared about me and you were really
telling the truth when you said you were looking for a solid
relationship with someone you could trust, then we wouldn't be
having this conversation.

DEE   This relationship turned into something I hadn't counted
on.

SYLVIE   Oh, really?  In what respect?

DEE   I didn't know I had to deal with your deep seeded
problems.

SYLVIE   My problems!  I've been used as your personal sounding board for months.  How you were ignored as a child...having a mother who left you emotionally barren, who never instilled you with self confidence...having brothers who were pampered while you got the shitty end of the stick.  Having a husband you don't sleep with and can't relate to and a job that has you trapped like a wild beast.  I listened with BOTH ears because I cared...but it seems that there is a little lacking on your part in that department, Dee LORES.

DEE   Oh, suddenly we've become formal and it's Delores?

SYLVIE   Damn you!   Why do you do that?

DEE   What?

SYLVIE   Get me side-tracked so I can't finish my tirade with the flash and fury I was working into!

DEE   Maybe because I don't want to hear it!

SYLVIE   (*Mimics*)   Oh, maybe she doesn't want to hear it?  Well, excuse me Ms. Sensitivity but maybe it's time we both said exactly what we both know is true.

DEE   What...that you want to leave?  Well, damn it, I'm vulnerable too!  You know I'm having a hard time with my life...and my mother DID abandon me emotionally...and now you're doing the same thing.

SYLVIE   Don't lay a guilt trip on me, Dee!  I won't fall for that crap.  I'm not playing "the game" with you anymore.  You don't play fair.

DEE   I just don't trust you, Sylvie.  I feel like I don't know anything about you.  You're so unpredictable.

SYLVIE   Well, that is certainly no basis for a relationship is it?

DEE   Relationship?  What is that?

SYLVIE   Exactly, Dee.  You don't care about me...you never did.  I don't get any feedback from you!

DEE   (*Playful*)   What...you don't like a little static in your life?

SYLVIE   No!  I need the clarity of a CD player not an old crystal radio set.  I also need someone with a little patience...to help me work out all these freakin' problems I'm facing.

DEE   Freaking is a perfect expletive, Sylvie.  I think I'm getting bored with your whinning.

SYLVIE   You are so fucking insensitive.  I can't deal with your attitude.  You are living in la la land.

DEE   (*Sing-song*)   It's the only place to dwell when the reality of your real life is hell...

SYLVIE   Dee, you make your own hell.  You wouldn't recognize Utopia if you fell over it.  You can't believe someone could actually love you.

DEE   Love?  Say that word again; I love it when you talk dirty.

SYLVIE   Stop it...I don't want to play.

DEE   Then what do you want?

SYLVIE   It doesn't matter anymore.  You don't believe what I say so why are you expecting an answer?

DEE   I always expect answers...you're the answer maven and I'm the expert interrogator (*German accent*)  Now, mein schatzie, vat do you experience from mein qvestions und how do you channel your emotions?

SYLVIE   Damn it!  Don't try to analyze me!  I get enough of that from my therapist.  Look, Dee...this conversation is going absolutely nowhere and so are we.

DEE   So, you just walk away?

SYLVIE   Well...you claim I fade in and out all the time so maybe I'll do must that.  Fade like the spotlight I'm bathed in right now.

(*Spotlight fades.*)

◆◆◆◆◆◆◆◆◆◆◆◆◆◆◆◆◆◆◆◆◆◆◆◆◆◆◆◆◆◆◆◆◆◆◆◆◆◆◆◆◆

**LYNN EMIDIA, born in Newark, New Jersey, started her theatrical career at a young age.  Lynn's mother was the first woman to produce and direct a live variety show on television in the '50's.  She explains, "I was born in a backstage trunk.  The first time I was on stage I was five.  One night the band played a familiar song.  Mother handed me the microphone, saying, 'Now sing!'"  Lynn sang, played piano, acted and directed in the theatre since that time and has never stopped, even though she married and had three children.  She attributes her versatility to a culturally enriched background - her father is a Sicilian Catholic and her mother, a Russian, German Jew.  Following a divorce eighteen years ago, she continued creative persuits through writing.  Her play has won local acclaim as part of a playwright series; she has participated in LACE Productions, a NJ Lesbian theatre group.**

**PEACE**

*Photos by Monique Frugier*

**GOING ON**

Photo by Ana R. Kissed

*"I see green blue eyes, a slender face and dark eyebrows...*
*I see movement and change...tides and a smile like leaves.*
*I see pain and happiness, little teeth, strength and*
*creativity...a mother, a child, a lover, a friend, my sister."*
*~ THRU THESE GLASSES WE'VE SEEN*
*OURSELVES EACH OTHER A LOOKING GLASS*

# *thru these glasses*
# *We've seen OurSelves*
# *Each Other a looking glass*
## *by Caitlin C. Cain*

**CHARACTERS** (In Order of Appearan:e):

ANNIE STEWART

GIRL

FEMALE VOICE

SHADOW

TAMARA SCALES

WOMYN

LUCIA

THE ACTION takes place in the present.

AT CURTAIN, *the stage is dark, bare and silent. Extended stillness gives way to a light from behind unfolding* ANNIE STEWART *at center stage.*

ANNIE   Caligula wanted to catch the moon, cage the impossible.  They thought he was mad, called him absurd.  I think he was selfish...really quite...dumb.  I want to pull the

33

moon out of me, suck it clear out of my sky...the real the raw...all that's naked. Grab it with both my hands, these hands; feel it seep between my fingers - breathing...alive. I want to raise it above my head and let it go...just let is fall...no cages...no struggle...still, like quiet. That's all. It's all I want...all I've ever wanted.

*(Stage goes black, lights up showing ANNIE sitting, huddled and rocking at stage left. She is next to her cluttered desk which rests on top of a crumpled mexican blanket. To her right is a tape recorder with various tapes and tape cases surrounding it. to her left lays a full ashtray, pack of cigarettes and a lighter. A bare mattress is off, diagonally, stage right.)*

ANNIE  *(Places cigarette in her mouth, lights it; inhaling, exhaling.)* None of us are the same - many of us are different, other. Some of us think we're adopted, some of us are...others think they're from Mars...another planet. I come from the sea, like a fish...and I always knew I was different...even as a little girl...mostly then...nothing fit...I couldn't say...why or how...I wasn't right inside.

*(GIRL enters, from stage right. ANNIE is unaware.)*

GIRL  *(Calling to off stage right.)* Goodnight Mommy...goodnight Daddy.

FEMALE VOICE  *(off stage right.)* Nitty-night Annie Marie...don't forget your prayers.

*(ANNIE reaches to tape recorder, plays soft blues...begins to sway about the stage. Girl walks to bed mattress, stares down.)*

ANNIE  *(Dancing, cigarette in hand.)* How did that go?

34

(*Dances over to* GIRL, *circling mattress*)  Now I lay me (GIRL *joins in, now kneeling at bed*)   down to sleep...if I die...

(GIRL *continues to pray silently.*)

ANNIE   (*Crosses back stage left, sits on desk*)   before I...I can't ...remember how far I got...(GIRL *crawls onto mattress, curls into a ball*)...my soul to keep...

(*Soft tapping from off stage right.*)

ANNIE   ...it was always then...every night...every week; all those years...

SHADOW   (*Whispering.  Off stage right*)   Annie? Annie...where's my pumpkin...hello button.

(SHADOW *enters stage right.  It has a wrapped box in its hands...trying to be quiet, it is stumbling about.*)

ANNIE   ...he always came then...well, not exactly then...he came into my bedroom then...always with a gift...see, Daddy's muffin, that's what he called me...had small tight openings...soaked with butter, hot out of the oven, I had a little mouth...little ears and big wide eyes...now I lay me down to sleep...I never got to finish...I never finished the prayer...

(SHADOW *kneels at mattress.  Puts wrapped box on the floor.* ANNIE *reaches for another smoke.*)

SHADOW   Annie...I brought you something, Muffin.  It's tiny and beautiful...like you shiny and special.   (GIRL *sits up in bed.* SHADOW *and* GIRL *embrace.*)

ANNIE   I was his favorite...he said so.  He'd let me sit in the front seat of his big blue car.  He bought me anything I wanted, everything I wanted...square presents, big presents; gifts for my smile, surprises for my little hands.  He said he was my own private santa claus...said I got to see him every night because he didn't live on the north pole...just between the two of us...he called me lucky, so did everyone else.  His clients thought I was lucky, they all called him santa too.  We used to deliver boxes of candy to them...they were old and in nursing homes.  I would sing christmas carols or play the piano...I used to wish I could stay there too...have my own room in that home of old ladies in white gowns.  I didn't know they were being killed too - that we were all dying.  Mom used to joke that one day all those old wimmin would just drop off the edge of the earth...then dad would have to stay home with her...and they'd be rich, having settled all those estates.  He never said that.  Everyone told us we looked alike.

*(SHADOW lets go of girl.  Exits stage right.  GIRL curls up on mattress.)*

ANNIE   *(Puts cigarette out.  Steps off desk and flips tape in recorder.  Sits on rug.)*   I used to have these dreams, one in particular...I still have it.  *(Stands crossing to center stage.)* I'm in this huge wheat field...I'm alone and it feels as though I'm standing on a zillion sewing needles, sharp points up...like your feet feel...just before they go to sleep.  All of a sudden, the whole field turns blood red and hot, like fire.  I look behind me and there are these troops, millions of them...and they have these long thin knives on top of their guns.  Soon, I'm surrounded by all these people...not soldiers...sort of familiar people, but I don't know them.  We start running...*(Crosses stage right, picks up the wrapped box, holds it in her hands)*...but there's this huge cement wall in front of us...as tall and wide as I can see.  As we're

*36*

running, a thick rope drops from the sky...it's attached to an air balloon. I hold the knot at the end while everyone starts climbing. (*Crosses stage left, puts wrapped box on her desk.*) Finally, it's my turn...I'm the last one. I reach the edge of the balloon basket and that's when I wake up.

(*Girl darts up straight, begins to scream and cry.*)

FEMALE VOICE   (From off stage right)   Annie, is that you? Sssshhh...Daddy's coming...

(*ANNIE crosses to stage right, bends down to crying GIRL. As she's about to embrace her, there is a knock from stage left. ANNIE stands, crosses to center stage. GIRL jumps up, runs off to stage right.*)

GIRL   (*Off stage right*)   Mommy...daddy...

ANNIE   (*Toward stage left*)   Come in...

(*Enter TAMARA SCALES, stage left. She is carrying an old, heavy typewriter.*)

TAMARA   (*Breathing heavily*)   Thanks for the type-write, Annie. (*Places typewriter on desk. Crosses to ANNIE*).   I really appreciate it. (*ANNIE spins away from TAMARA.*) Well...guess I won't try to thank you. (*Glancing around desk...TAMARA is looking at various papers.*)

ANNIE   (*Noticing*)   See something you like?

TAMARA   (*Turns to ANNIE*)   I see a lot of things I like...

ANNIE   (*Quick*)   You wanna smoke? Cup of tea? I've got

your tapes over there...you can -

TAMARA   (*Interrupts*)  Annie, I just came to bring the
typewriter...you can keep the tapes for a while
longer...(*Sitting*)...how are you?

ANNIE   (*Pacing*)   How am I?  I got two crank calls last night,
my mother sent socks...I can't find any crayons -

TAMARA   (*Interrupts*)...you, Annie...I asked how you are.

ANNIE   (Sitting)  Me.  (Silence)  Hi.

TAMARA   Hi.

ANNIE   How's it goin?

TAMARA   Annie...

ANNIE   Got any stories?

TAMARA   Nope...no stories tonight.

ANNIE   Come on...not even a little one?

TAMARA   (*Standing*)   Nothing's a little anymore, Annie - it's
all big - huge, actually...sometimes, I think -

ANNIE   (*Interrupts*)   - so darn serious...

TAMARA   (*Angry*)  ...it is serious, this is important to
me...you're important to me...the way I feel about you isn't some
story -

ANNIE   (*Interrupts*)   - just talk to me...entertain me...I don't
have a t.v. and I can't afford the movies.

TAMARA   You must be busy on some project or
something...some big love epic - the entrails of your mind -
everything real, remember that, Annie.  You -

ANNIE   (*Interrupts*)   - I write all the time...scenes, poems,
novels...it's all in here.  (*Motions to her head.*)

TAMARA   (*Kneeling at* ANNIE's *side*)   Silly girl,
Annie...(*Motions to* ANNIE's *chest*)  ...it should be in here...this
is where you come from...not up here.  (*Reaches for Annie's
forehead*)   You know, I -

ANNIE   (*Stands quickly, interrupts*)   - what do you mean silly.

TAMARA   (*Standing. Frustrated*)   Silly means lots of
things...at lots of times...

ANNIE   So...you're not gonna tell me?

TAMARA   You already know, Annie - you know lots of
things...I just don't get to know about them -

ANNIE   (*Interrupts*)   - don't believe in me so much...Tamara, I
can't - I don't know how...

TAMARA   (*Interrupts*)   - hey, Annie - don't say don't...and
please don't say can't.  Why don't you tell me a story...put
yourself in it...surprise me for once - tell me -

ANNIE   (*Defensive*)   - I asked you first.

TAMARA   When?

ANNIE   When you walked in...I asked you to entertain me, remember?

TAMARA   Wouldn't want to break the rules, would I?  Annie, I'm tired...I don't wanna play...I don't want to keep doing -

ANNIE   (*Interrupts*)   - what do you mean play?

TAMARA   You know what you mean.

ANNIE   You think this is a game, don't you?

TAMARA   I know -

ANNIE   (*Interrupts*)   - it's not, you know I -

TAMARA   (*Interrupts*)   - Annie - don't you ever get tired? Sick of carrying around all this excess baggage?  They're feelings, Annie...and they're important - because they're yours...and because they're mine.

ANNIE   (*Ignoring her*)   You're thirty-seven years old...living in the Village, above a bakery on Christopher Street.

TAMARA   Hey, Annie...this is me...I'm nineteen years old...I just got my first D...

ANNIE   (*Interrupts*)   ...come on, please - just one...

TAMARA   Do I have to?  (*Pacing*)  What's so wrong here? Can't we just stay here for a change...in this room, on this floor...that's where we are, you know?  This is Bradford Hall and

40

we're on the sixth floor...we're not in New York City - walking down the street with a loaf of bread under one arm and a poetry book in the other.

ANNIE   How do you know I'm not bringing home flowers for you?

TAMARA   Oh, Annie - listen to you...*(Crosses to desk, picks up wrapped box)*...belated birthday?

ANNIE   Don't touch that...

TAMARA   *(Turns to her. Shakes box)*   Umm...it's a sailboat...a box of cereal?

ANNIE   I'm serious...put it back.

TAMARA   A mountain bike?  The complete Billie Holiday collection - on disc.

ANNIE   *(Takes box from Tamara, places it on desk)*   That's enough.

TAMARA   *(Facing her. Long silence)*   Well...you are here afterall.  I can still bring you back...welcome home, you.  How was New York?  Go shopping?  What did you have for lunch?  *(Pause)*   I worry, Annie...that's all...when I can't reach you, I get to missing you.

ANNIE   What do you want?  What's with you?

TAMARA   I want to tell you something - something real.  No metaphors, no prose...move me, Annie - touch me with your words...your words about you - what you dream about, what you

*41*

feel...what you did today. I don't know where you are half of the time. You always talk to me or at me, never with me...about you, about me - about us.

ANNIE    Us? It's not important.

TAMARA    Thanks.

ANNIE    I mean, what's in the box, it's not important.

TAMARA    I didn't - it's not about pushing, Annie...there's not a shove, only sharing.

ANNIE    For all I know...it's empty.

TAMARA    What do you mean? Didn't you wrap it? You wrapped an empty box.

ANNIE    Very carefully. *(Picks up wrapped box)*    See the corners...you can barely tell they're sealed - I put the tape on the inside...You know, so you couldn't see it, the shiny stuff, I mean.

TAMARA    Enough about the box, Annie. We need to talk about you.

ANNIE    *(Puts box back on desk)*    I do tell you about me. I am telling you about me. Aren't you listening?

TAMARA    Alright...*(Facing her, reaches for her hands)*...I want to tell a story...and I want you to listen very carefully because I'm not gonna tell it again. Do you understand?

ANNIE    You're giving into peer pressure.

**Photo by Ana R. Kissed**

*"She is sifting through debris around her..."*

43

TAMARA  No...speaking your language - playing your game. *(Stands. Crosses center stage.)*  You're in Chicago...visiting your cousin or something -

ANNIE  *(Interrupts.)*  - Cindy lives in Arizona.

TAMARA  Don't interrupt.  You're walking down the street - it's raining out and you're soaking wet.  You don't care, but you worry about the bagels you just bought - the bag they're in is soggy and falling apart.  You see this tiny theatre, nestled between a health food store and a stationery shop.  You grab a bag of fig bars and enter the theatre.  You're not so interested in the play, you just want to dry off. *(Raises her arms, dropping them slowly, bringing stage lights down.)*  The stage is dark.  You're in the third row. *(House lights go on, stage is still dark. TAMARA and ANNIE are unseen.)*  Just as the house lights go down (house lights down), you remember you're supposed to meet Cindy's friend for lunch...You're about to leave as the stage lights up...*(stage lights up showing WOMYM sitting on bed mattress stage right.  Around her are stacks of both books and papers, pencils and pens are everywhere.  She is sifting through the debris surrounding her.  TAMARA and ANNIE are not present)*...there's this womyn sitting on a bare mattress sifting through oddles of short stories, dialogue and poetry.  You wonder if she's written it all herself or someone else has...whether you can meet her.  You wanna read all her work, get to know her.  She's bold and that draws you to her - she makes you feel less alone.  You're glad you stayed.

WOMYN  *(Holding bits and pieces of paper.  Paces, crumples paper, tosses it across the room.  Paces.)*  Our kitchen is quiet, not so fun...much pain and I'm alone here...neglected like the toast, burnt, four pieces resting on each other, but in half.  My tea is familiar, unlike you, unlike us...brown sugar and soy milk.

TAMARA  *(from off stage)*  you like thinking about her
kitchen, wonder why she drinks tea and not coffee.  It's only
been five minutes but you feel like you've known this womyn
your whole life.  You love the tone of her voice, the way she
moves...you have to keep reminding yourself - it's
dialogue...you're in a theatre...she's an actress, Annie.  What
you're hearing isn't real - the words weren't written by her or for
you.

WOMYN  *(Reading)*  She was a collage - like browns or
greens...an orange like Fall...nobody knew her - not even me...I
guessed about her while she wrote about me.

TAMARA  *(From off stage)*  Suddenly, another womyn jumps
up from a seat in the audience.  (ANNIE *jumps up from a seat
in the audience)*  She begins to clap her hands.  She walks on
stage.  (ANNIE *walks on stage)*  You get to feeling nervous,
like you've walked in on a private rehearsal.

ANNIE  *(Center stage, facing* WOMYN *clapping)*
Excellent...that's great.  *(Shakes* WOMYN*'s hand)*  Thanks for
your time...I'll let you know how it goes.

WOMYN  *(Passing papers to* ANNIE*)*  I was sorta scared -
I'm not really the performin' type...you know, nerves.

*TAMARA  (From off stage)*  You're shattered.  You feel
cheated, ripped off.  A pretty pattern, Annie - words arranged to
fit someone else's warped puzzle.  You were touched though,
moved by what you could feel for this womyn, this character...at
least you thought you were.

ANNIE  Go and get something to eat...I'll call you tonight.

WOMYN   Alright, thanks.

ANNIE   (*Alone on stage; crosses to desk, puts papers next to wrapped box. Stared down at it.*)   I was moved...

TAMARA   (*Off stage*)   you wait till everyone leaves, smoke a cigarette in the lobby, toss your bagels in the ashtray and leave the theatre...

(*Stage lights up,* TAMARA *and* ANNIE *as before.*)

TAMARA   ...what are you thinking?

ANNIE   That I shouldn't have bought bagels on a rainy day?

TAMARA   (*Crossing to* ANNIE. *Long silence*)   You break my heart...your silence is so...deafening...and, you can't see.

ANNIE   I don't wanna hurt you...honest.

TAMARA   Then stop hurting yourself, Annie.  I'm not here to hinder you...I'm here to help you grow and to love you - I want to be a part of your life and want you to be a part of mine...but I'm all alone here...you refuse to help me, refuse to help yourself ...I deserve better, Annie and so do you...I thought you knew that. (*Stands, exits stage left.*)

ANNIE   (*Silence. Standing.  Goes to desk, grabs wrapped box. Crosses stage right to mattress.  Sits.  Places box between her feet, reaches into her pocket and pulls a piece of paper.  Pulls phone from behind mattress.  Dials.  Pause.*) Hello...Hi...my name is Annie, Annie Stewart.  I think I need to talk to someone...with someone. (*Stage lights down.*)

**Photo by Ana R. Kissed**

*"She takes chances, she free falls into darkness..."*

ANNIE   *(From somewhere on stage)*   It's funny sometimes - the way things work out.  Here I was so small alone and vulnerable calling some crumbled number I carried around since orientation...The Wimmin's Center...it all sounded so scarey to me...all I could see were girls from high school talking about zits and football players.  I called...because I understood...I finally saw how brave Tamara is.  She takes chances, she free falls into darkness...with nothing to go on but the hope I'll love her back. I let her down...I couldn't share...she left before I told her to...

*(The stage lights up to show* ANNIE *sitting cross-legged, on the floor, across from* LUCIA.  *Between them is* ANNIE'*s wrapped box.)*

LUCIA   So, this is great...we finally meet...

ANNIE   ...yea, we have bodies now...to go with our voices. Good thing you don't live two states away.

LUCIA   We all have bodies...beautiful strong bodies.

ANNIE   Have you...have you always...

LUCIA   ...always...I've ALWAYS been a Dyke, Annie, ain't no knobby-kneed prick sharin' my live, you bet!!

ANNIE   Hey, I'm the angry one, remember?

LUCIA   Angry...hell, Annie, I'm ragin' -

ANNIE   - a ragin' -

LUCIA   - courageous -

ANNIE AND LUCIA  - AMAZON!

LUCIA   That's right.

ANNIE   I'm sorry I hung up on you.

LUCIA   Which time, Annie?

ANNIE   It was only twice...once when you said I should think -

LUCIA   - it was six times.  And everytime had to do with me calling you on somethinig.

ANNIE   Come on...I'm not so bad, Lucia...I just -

LUCIA   I know...you're working on it...you're gonna get it right soon...you get nervous...

ANNIE   ...I do...

LUCIA   ...please, poor Annie - calls the Wimmin's Center...finally...and zoom - enter big bad, and I am, Lucia...who, by the way, just happened to be there...answering the phones for Shelly.

ANNIE   Speaking of which -

LUCIA   - let's not.

ANNIE   Lucia...

LUCIA   ...alright...well...let's just say some wimmin make decisions and some set priorities...me, I set priorities...so, I've made a couple lousy decisions...but, I know who's side I'm on I'll

*49*

tell you that much...spread the word, work to change it...wimmin don't know.

ANNIE   Know what?

LUCIA   That we can make choices - that we create movement...that we exist...real and alive - we breathe - here and now.

ANNIE   Some wimmin like -

LUCIA   - oh blahblah yeahyeah, just like some wimmin like radioactive sludge, nuclear fallout and gang rape.

ANNIE   Lucia...do you hate your father?

LUCIA   Damn right I do.

ANNIE   Do you ever...do you ever get...

LUCIA   ...scared?

ANNIE   Yeah.

LUCIA   I get scared lots of times.

ANNIE   What do you do?

LUCIA   Play Alix Dobkin...turn on a light...slice a bag of onions.

ANNIE   Onions?

LUCIA   Helps me cry.

ANNIE   Maybe I should try that.

LUCIA   Annie...none of this is easy...most of it sucks - it's awful to feel terrified...to doubt yourself...I'm furious at him, at them, at the pollution they've erected in schools and homes on playgrounds...it makes us less...makes us useable...fuckable...I'll never be five again or ten or thirteen...and neither will you.

ANNIE   I feel little...I feel touchable...like he's gonna get me.

LUCIA   You've learned things, Annie...you're older now...and stronger.  You can go back there on your own terms...

ANNIE   ...I don't ever want to see him again...I told you that last month, Lucia...don't you hear me?

LUCIA   Whoa, Annie...hold up...this is me here and I was talking about being scared because you asked me about fear...which got me angry...then, I started talking about how we aren't children anymore -

ANNIE   - I don't need an overview, Lucia...I asked if you listen to me.

LUCIA   Hey, Annie - I'm not Tamara...and I'm not gonna -

ANNIE   - I asked a question...I just want -

LUCIA   - yes, Annie...yes, I listen with you...start listening with me and the both of us will hear more clearly.  I'm trying to tell you that while you never have to see your father again, as you told me last week, not last month...we go back there - all the time...we go back to those bedrooms and we see those walls and we touch those windowpanes...and, yes...we see him and we feel

*51*

his hands and we smell his breath...but, Annie, that's not us anymore...we're here - we got out...we got away...and we go back on our terms, not his...we can fight back and we can scream...we know more - you know -

ANNIE   - Lucia...I don't know so much...I can't put it together yet...you're further along...don't you see that - you're at a different place...I can't -

LUCIA   - don't say -

ANNIE   - can't...and don't say don't...oh Lucia...this is such a drag...my mother called yesterday...she doesn't even know.

LUCIA   I dunno, Annie - please be careful...

ANNIE   ...Lucia -

LUCIA   ...Annie...where was their room?

ANNIE   Their room was upstairs, Lucia, Okay?  What do you want me to say...my mother screwed me too?

LUCIA   Annie, hey, I just want you to take some time.

ANNIE   Back off Lucia -

LUCIA   - come on...I don't deserve that...you don't talk a lot about your mom...maybe that has to do with -

ANNIE   - our mothers are different -

LUCIA   - alright, alright...it's true...your mother and my mother are not the same...but most hallways are not so long and most walls are not so thick -

ANNIE   - I don't know who knows, Lucia...I don't know who knew.

LUCIA   This isn't a trial, Annie...

ANNIE   Why do you stick around anyway; what's in it for you?

LUCIA   I'm here because we need to be heard...we want to be understood...it gushes out of us - like the ocean or clouds in the sky...we're breaking all the silences, Annie...we're finally getting our day, our time to be honest with each other with ourselves, we need one another, Annie...survivors need each other.

ANNIE   I don't want to need you.

LUCIA   Ouch.

ANNIE   And, I don't want to be figured out.

LUCIA   Liar.

ANNIE   Lying is useful, you said it yourself.

LUCIA   Lies can be used, in some instances, for protection...that is, if some creep asks for your address...and you feel pressured for an answer.  Lying helped me survive...but, I don't lie to us...I don't lie to wimmin and I don't lie to survivors.

ANNIE   I don't want to lie to you.

LUCIA   Then don't Annie, if you think you can get further out without taking time to look inside, you're wrong.

53

ANNIE   Out where, Lucia?  Where is out; what's out all about?

LUCIA   Exactly.  Out and about...zipping through the cosmos...tripping through and beyond time ... shapeshifting...you've got to read Mary Daly.

ANNIE   Read Mary Daly, listen to Ova, hug an armful of leaves...write messages in the sunset...I can't keep up with you.

LUCIA   Out is wild...out is untamed...you know this, Annie...it's not about keeping up, it's about coming along...come along with me.

ANNIE   My mother isn't your mother.

LUCIA   Right...it's true...you didn't write a note to your mother in the sand on a beach...daddy fucks me; you weren't slapped into the tide as it was washed away...that's true...we come from the same place, don't you see?  Annie...we've been doing this for months now...you've been calling me every night -

ANNIE   - every other night.

LUCIA   Every night for a long time now and we've been sharing...like I said, breaking silences...again, creating movement...propelling each other, gathering strength.

ANNIE   I called because of Tamara.

LUCIA   Tamara...you called for a lot of reasons, but let's talk about Tamara.

ANNIE   Let's not.

LUCIA   Why don't you call her?

ANNIE   I'm scared.

LUCIA   I know, probably a little weary too...the actress thing,
right?  Well, so you ask wimmin to tell you stories a lot ...you're
not too good at talking about yourself...you're getting better,
Annie...and Tamara's smart...give her credit...give yourself credit.

ANNIE   I told her not to believe in me.

LUCIA   Of course you did.  No one's supposed to believe
us...and, quite frequently, no one does believe us...that's why we
think we're crazy.

ANNIE   You're not so smart.

LUCIA   I am too.  See, Annie...Tamara's got something figured
out.

ANNIE   Lucia, you don't even know her.

LUCIA   Not yet...but, this is what the deal is...she knows
wimmin aren't afraid of pain or death...we've been so fucked
over, our ability to withstand pain is is great that we can't even
feel when we're in pain...we're so numbed out and so mixed up
by all the snools and their death loving world, we're scared fo
life...we're scared of what's real and genuine...what moves us to
feel rage and joy and love and sorrow.

ANNIE   She's gotta hate me.

LUCIA   Wimmin don't hate each other...quite often, we hate
ourselves...all those repetitive objectives; whore slit gash bitch

*55*

cunt...they seep in...we're suckered into believing them...and when we try to help each other...sometimes we make bad choices...we hurt each other and ourselves.

ANNIE  (*Crossing to wrapped box*)  I want to give you something.  (*Hands* LUCIA *box.*)

LUCIA  (*Taking box*)  Hhuummm...why now, Annie...why me?

ANNIE  Whatya mean?

LUCIA  I mean...do you feel like you should give me something.  Or...do you want to give me something...I don't know what this means.

ANNIE  It doesn't mean anything...I wanted to give you a little something because...because you've helped me out a lot and I thought I should...

LUCIA  (Handing back box)  - I thought so...keep it.

ANNIE  Well, wait a minute...no one gives gifts back...I mean some effort went into it, it's not, I don't know...it's not a -

LUCIA  - Annie...if it doesn't mean anything -

ANNIE  - I didn't mean -

LUCIA  - Well, what did you mean?

ANNIE  Lucia, come on...I can't be completely concise all the time...

LUCIA  Say what you mean, Annie - it's safe here...I don't want

*56*

something from you that doesn't mean anything and I don't want to be given something with the expectation of getting something back...gifts are special...I know it's confusing for you.

ANNIE   My father...alright, I tried to forget it -

LUCIA   - give it to yourself, Annie...for real, for once; give yourself something.

ANNIE   you know...I don't get it (*standing...pacing*)   I mean, who talks to a complete stranger for six months...I could be straight for all you know...maybe I made the whole story up...maybe I'm from the school newspaper and I'm gonna print a big story about you and your -

LUCIA   - don't do this Annie...don't be stupid -

ANNIE   - see, now I'm stupid...next I'll be nuts, you've already called me a liar -

LUCIA   - keep it up, Annie...it's great to get angry and it's important to feel rage, to be courageous -

ANNIE   - I am brave -

LUCIA   -yet, you are, Annie...you are brave, but you're coming close to forgetting something real vital.

ANNIE   And what's that smarty?

LUCIA   Never forget what you're fighting for, Annie and never forget what you're fighting against...but most importantly...never ever forget who you fight with...I'm not the enemy...

ANNIE   And am I?

LUCIA   Come on.

ANNIE   I gotta go   *(moves to exit stage right)* ..this is just too-

LUCIA   *(Walking toward* ANNIE*)* - Annie, I'll be honest with you...*(handing box to* ANNIE*)*...if you walk out that door, you're gonna have to go back to square one with me...

ANNIE   - What does that mean?

LUCIA   It means that I'll remember these past months...everything we've worked on and I'll continue to weave us into my life, but...I will not have wimmin in my space working against me...I want community...and I know it's not easy...there are lots and lots of differences...we come from both different and similar places...I want to create a common focus out of many wimmin's unique selves...I won't have reversals spit out at me.

ANNIE   I don't always understand you...I don't know what to do, Lucia...I don't know where to start and I don't know who is to trust.

LUCIA   You can start with me...me and Tamara...

ANNIE   ...you don't -

LUCIA   - I know...I don't even know her.

ANNIE   No you don't...not yet.

LUCIA   So...what do you say, Annie?

*58*

ANNIE   *(Lights fading.)*   You got a garbage can?

LUCIA   No Sep would be without one.

ANNIE   Well...*(Tosses box to LUCIA)*...then this is for you. *(Stage dark. ANNIE continues to speak.)*  So I did it...I let her in...it wasn't as bad as I thought...just like Tamara said, "It's not so lousy being loved."  I get scared...I'm still scared...Lucia gets scared too...she's pretty bold though...like that actress...all these wimmin...they're so brave...and me, me feels small...I'm disappointed in me...and I'm tired, tired of running - darting into buildings, hiding behind trees...I've done everything to stay away...away from me, away from Tamara...I wanna cry...I think I'll call instead.

*(Stage lights up to ANNIE's room as before. Knock from stage left.)*

ANNIE   Come in.  (E*nter TAMARA from stage left. She is carrying the same wrapped box as earlier shown.)*

TAMARA   *(Tossing box on ANNIE's bed.)*   Here...it's old...I got it last year...I'm sick of looking at it -

ANNIE   *(Sitting on rug)*   - will you come here?

TAMARA   *(Pacing)*  So...I'm curious...did you open my letters?

ANNIE   Yes.

TAMARA   Good material, huh?  I'm sure -

ANNIE   Tamara -

*59*

TAMARA   - there's got to be a couple of plays in there...lots of love poems...probably even a book -

ANNIE   (*Stands, crossing to* TAMARA.)  I know you're -

TAMARA   (*Spins away, crosses stage left*)  - don't.  (*Pause*) No, Annie...you don't know...you don't know what it feels like...I'm not a child...I have integrity...I have respect for myself...I came here because -

ANNIE   - you deserve answers.

TAMARA   Stop interrupting me.  Yea...I want answers...I wanna know why you leave - pack up, move on - drop out, disappear...why I'm always on the outside..(ANNIE *sits)*...why you're so determined to...be alone.

ANNIE   We're all alone.

TAMARA   (*Kneeling, taking* ANNIE's *face.*)  I just wanted to know you...couldn't you tell...I was so patient with you...

ANNIE   ...I know that now...

TAMARA   ...oh...shit... (*Stands, pacing*)...damnit, Tammy...why do you do this?  Why do you always care for the ones who don't care back?

ANNIE   I care.

TAMARA   (*Ignoring* ANNIE.)  Why do you always want to be near the ones who don't want to be near you?

ANNIE   I wanna be near you.

TAMARA  *(Ignoring* ANNIE.*)*  I mean...what is it with you...it's so boring...it's repetitive...it's painful...everyone's so scared...everyone's so...dead -

ANNIE  *(Crosses to* TAMARA.*)*  - I'm alive...I'm here...I breathe...I love you...I'm sorry, Tamara...please -

TAMARA  *(Spins away)*  - act one, scene two...I'm sorry, Tamara...I love you, please forgive me, Tamara -

ANNIE  - I tell my own story now -

TAMARA  - acting them out...being an act-

ANNIE  -ress. *(Pause)*  It's easier to be someone else...I hurt being me...I threw in things that didn't matter...I spent this whole relationship -

TAMARA  - are you defining something, Annie...because I'm not part of your definition...not anymore...I wrote you that I loved you...I don't love you anymore -

ANNIE  - you're lying -

TAMARA  - watch it, Annie.

ANNIE  *(Crosses to box, picks it up.)*  Let me tell you about these...can I?

TAMARA  I don't know...can you?

ANNIE  I used to think it was a gift.  a pretty box someone else always got to open up before me.  See...I got used to it...I got so used to being wrapped up, dressed for an occasion...I forgot about myself...I forgot who I -

TAMARA   - was.  Obviously...Annie, I'm right here...I'm not a piece of paper...trash the metaphors...what are you tryiing to say?

ANNIE   I wanna share.

TAMARA   Then do it...do the right thing.

ANNIE   I've been a lousy friend.

TAMARA   Yeah, Annie, you have.

ANNIE   I had a responsibility...to you to me...to us...I blew off everything I felt for you -

TAMARA   - You always did that.

ANNIE   No...I didn't...*(crosses to desk)*...it's all here... *(grabs stacks of paper.)*  Poems don't talk back...characters don't leave and daddy never fucks you in your stories...daddy is nice and gentle and comes home from work and mommy and you  have dinner...and you all watch t.v. and you fall asleep on the couch and mommy puts you to bed and you wake up in the morning... and school is okay and you like everyone else...and daddy doesn't give you presents all the time...tell you to keep secrets...call you his favorite girl...my stories don't have daddies-

TAMARA   *(Crossing to* ANNIE*)*   - hey, Annie...I know...

ANNIE   ...your mom's a Dyke...you never knew your dad -

TAMARA   - but I know all about him...all about them...

ANNIE   - your father never fucked you -

TAMARA   - no, he didn't...he raped my mother and he raped her mother...and they killed him.

ANNIE   *(Long pause)*   What?

TAMARA   My mothers killed my father...

ANNIE   ...are they in jail?

TAMARA   Annie...it's a small town...he was a real bastard...everyone hated him...he drank a lot...they did something to his car...he went to a bar and never came home...Alice lives with my mom...she's the only doctor around...her sister teaches the children...their mother runs the town...they took my mother in...my grandmother appreciated them...she hated my father...no one asked questions.

ANNIE   That's the most amazing -

TAMARA   - a real life story, Annie - no paper, no pens...just hard work...cunning and lots of wit.

ANNIE   Why didn't you tell me?

TAMARA   Why didn't I tell you?  You said it yourself...you're learning...you haven't always known.

ANNIE   Yea...but -

TAMARA   - yea but nothing...I didn't trust you...I still don't trust you.

ANNIE   Square one, huh?

TAMARA   Not exactly...I don't forget easily...my mothers have taught me too well, "always remember", they say...never forget...

ANNIE   - what we're fighting for?

TAMARA   Who we're fighting with...and for...

ANNIE   ...against.

TAMARA   yea, that too.

ANNIE   I've spent a lot of time forgetting...turning away, turning off.

TAMARA   I remember you...I remember the first day I met you...I remember your black beret and I remember green pants...I remember long nights...too many cigarettes. *(Pause)* Hey, do you have one?

ANNIE   I quit.

TAMARA   Whoa...I remember dark beer and drawing pictures...I remember your laugh...I remember knowing you were a survivor.

ANNIE   How?

TAMARA   You're mean to yourself...you think you're undeserving you flinch...you can't look me in the eyes.

ANNIE   I'm looking now.

TAMARA    Then everything became hips and calves and muscle. *(Long pause)*   I thought that meant something.

ANNIE   It did...it does.

TAMARA   I thought you let me in.

ANNIE   I couldn't   *(Long pause)* It's really gross...

TAMARA   ...thanks.

ANNIE   Not you...what I'm about to say...I can't say no...I can't say stop...I'm still sleeping with daddy.

TAMARA   Oh, Annie...I know what those things mean...I know what stop means...I know what no means...

ANNIE   How?

TAMARA   I listen with wimmin...I listen to our lives...I'm creating space...places to be safe...but I can't do that alone.

ANNIE   I wanna help...I wanna be there.

TAMARA   Then be here...make your father leave...he can't sit between us, he can't eat at our table...and he will not sleep between us.

ANNIE   I'm afraid of him.

TAMARA   I'm scared too...it's a filthy world.

ANNIE   There are beautiful things too.

TAMARA  That's right, Annie...there are.

ANNIE  Like trees and clouds and animals...
TAMARA  ...and the ocean and windy days...

ANNIE  ...and the rain...

TAMARA  ...and the sunshine...

ANNIE  and wimmin too?

TAMARA  And wimmin. *(Crosses to wrapped box, presents it to ANNIE.)* And these...gifts that mean something - given with strength and hope...gifts that don't require services...or a thank you card.

ANNIE  *(Takes box.)*  Where do you come from?

TAMARA  I come from right here...right here is where I am. ...You've got time Annie...it's gonna become clearer...the parts will come together - some in trickles, others in great bunches.

ANNIE  What about you...how much time do you have?

TAMARA  I haven't decided yet...maybe as much time as it takes for you to open this...maybe as much time as it takes for you to understand it.

ANNIE  *(Shaking the box.)*  It's a box of cereal...a mountain bike...the complete Billie Holiday collection -

TAMARA  - on disc?

ANNIE  Of course...*(Unwraps box, removes lid, peaks inside.)*

*66*

A new typewriter...just jokin' *(From the box* ANNIE *pulls a mirror. Long extended pause. Annie looks at* TAMARA.. ANNIE *looks into mirror.)*

TAMARA    This is...you...Okay?  I know it's hard for you to see who I see...this is the beginning...this is where you start.

ANNIE    So...what...do you see...who do you see?

TAMARA    I see green blue eyes, a slender face and dark eyebrows...I see movement and change...tides and a smile like leaves.    I see pain and happiness, little teeth, strength and creativity...a mother and a child, a lover and a friend, my sister. *(Long pause)*    Tell me, Annie...tell me what you see.

ANNIE    Umm...I see you...

TAMARA    ...and who else?

ANNIE    I see me...that's me...I'm right here...trying to learn and trying to love.

*(Stage dark.)*

◆◆◆◆◆◆◆◆◆◆◆◆◆◆◆◆◆◆◆◆◆◆◆◆◆◆◆◆◆◆◆◆◆◆◆◆◆◆

**CAITLIN C. CAIN'S one act play was written during her last year at New College of Hofstra University.  It was performed as a different version that year.  She says, "I've done quite a bit of work on it since then...introduced a Sep, made the father a shadow.  It's been really great for Me to reWork It...I've learned a lot about MySelf and My Writing /RightIng Self." Caitlin lives in Cape Cod with her five cats.**

**Memory of Elizabeth, Cross Stitch by Phyllis RoseChild**
*Photo by Sue McConnell-Celi*

# Portrait of Ana R. Kissed

**ANA R. KISSED**

*"I am a middle aged (47), white, working class, dyke separatist single mother of two now grown daughters whose choice of sexuality is not yet clear. I am a survivor of two hetero-patriarchal families - the one I was born into and the one I married into. I expect that healing from and celebrating my escape from my families will continue as long as I do. I am an artist. I work in many media, sometimes I write. I make money working in a group home for Adults with Developmental Disabilities. I keep myself alive making photographs and other art."*

"*Much of my art is a celebration of the existance of lesbians. I believe it is essential to record us in the dailyness of our lives. Most of the dykes I photograph, including myself, are or have been intimates, not necessarily lovers.*"

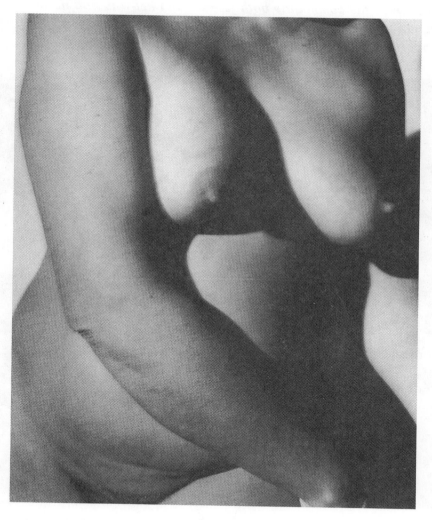

**Self-Portrait from WOMBYN OVER FORTY by Ana R. Kissed**

*"Last summer I again gloried in the experience of being at wombyn-only gatherings where we felt free enough to shed our clothes and go about without shame, revealing our bodies to each other. I took many photographs and shared with wombyn in the community both lesbian and het-who had never been in this kind of space. They were amazed at how comfortable we seemed in our nakedness."*

**CELEBRATION AT HOWL, Vermont    Photo by Ana R. Kissed**

**Myrna and Daisy, Twolights, '92 (top,L); Dykes from the East and from the West, Berlin, '90 (top,R); A Gathering in Vermont, '80's.**

*"These photos not only record the lives and existence of the dykes imaged...*

*...they often portray to us aspects of ourselves...and our relationships that we haven't perceived yet."* - **Ana R. Kissed**

**Exhibitions:** MAINE PHOTO BIENNIAL, 1984; SISTERS-SOLO Exhibit, 1985; "Women Over Forty Nude Photos, 1988 "Lesbian Art Show" - LESBIAN & GAY CENTER, NYC; "Portraits of Lesbians"- CRONES HARVEST, Boston, '92; "Looking At My Kind"-CRONES HARVEST, 1993.

# Womyn Of The Moon ~

**Woodcuts by Jacque Harper & Ruth Brose**

**Claywork of Cindy Hardin**       *Photo by Zel Bowers*

*"Beth, she's 17 years-old.*
*She said she wouldn't be home late, and I believed her."*
        - *COMING IN*

# COMING IN

## by Anne M. Harris

### CHARACTERS:

JOAN   *A forties-something lesbian.*

BETH   *Her lover, and the mother of their daughter,* APRIL.

APRIL   *A flouncy, 17 year-old.*

*Early morning. Lights up on* BETH *and* JOAN *sitting at the kitchen table eating breakfast.* JOAN *reads the paper. Beth tries nervously to eat some toast.*

BETH   *(Examining a wallclock.)*   It's nearly five a.m.

JOAN   *(Still reading.)*   Don't worry. She's fine.

BETH   Did she say who she was meeting?

JOAN   I, uh...I didn't ask.

BETH   What do you MEAN, you didn't ask?

JOAN   Beth, she's 17 years-old.  She said she wouldn't be home late, and I believed her.

BETH   Oh that was smart.

JOAN   Look, she's a very responsible kid -

BETH    - and responsible kids don't have hormones?

JOAN    I think you're overreacting...

*(The door opens, in walks their daughter* APRIL, *dressed for an evening out. She looks a little dishevelled, but otherwise happy and intact.)*

APRIL    Hi Mom!  Hi Joan!

BETH    *(To* JOAN*)*    She's not even afraid of us...

APRIL    What are you guys doing up so early?

BETH    Waiting for you.  Come here and sit down a minute.
*(Pulls out a chair,* APRIL *sits.)*

APRIL    What is it Mom?

BETH    Well, Joan and I love you very much.  You know that, don't you?

APRIL    Sure, Mom.

BETH    Well, we were just wondering if there's something you'd like to...talk about.    Anything at all?

JOAN    Like boys, for instance?

APRIL    BOYS?

JOAN    Yes.

APRIL    *(Fidgetting now.)*  W-Why would I want to talk about boys?

BETH   Well for heaven's sake, I don't know, it's just that - well, we've been noticing a few things, and -

APRIL   Noticing things?  Like what?

BETH   Well, for instance...the other day...we were all outside raking leaves, you remember?

APRIL   *(Defensively)*   Yeah, so?

BETH   ...and I was cutting down those saplings, and Joan was repairing the roof, and she asked you to...to mow the lawn, and -

APRIL   ...And I said I didn't want to, is that it?

BETH   Well, yeah, partly...

APRIL   So?  What is THAT supposed to mean?

BETH   *(Trying to stay calm.)*   Don't you remember what you said to me, honey?

APRIL   *(Defensive, not following this line.)*  No -

BETH   - YOU WERE AFRAID YOU'D BREAK A NAIL! *(Dissolves in tears.)*

JOAN   *(Comforting* BETH)   It's just that we've tried to raise you the best possible way...we've tried to convey our morals to you, our belief that everyone should be self-sufficient, capable...

APRIL   But I AM capable...

BETH  *(Still crying)*  ...and you haven't even TOUCHED those Birkenstocks I bought for you last week.  It's always mini-skirts, halter dresses...just tell me, April, where did we go wrong?

APRIL  You didn't go wrong!  It's just me...it has nothing to DO with you and Joan...I know you've done your best - and you've done a WONDERFUL job...but people are different. Like you've always told me:  it takes all kinds.

JOAN  I don't think this is what your mother and I had in mind when we said that.

BETH  Don't misunderstand, darling; I don't want you to think we're ashamed of you.  We're not really ASHAMED, but -

JOAN  What are we supposed to tell our friends?

APRIL  Tell them the TRUTH!

JOAN  *(Dismayed)*  Oh sure.

APRIL  Then lie; I don't care.  Tell them we're just friends. Tell them whatever you want.

BETH  They're not going to believe that crap!  They have eyes! Do you really think they're that stupid?  They see you in town with Billy!  How long do you think people are going to believe you're just 'friends'?

APRIL  Mom, look.  I'm not like this to HURT you and Joan. I don't know how it happened...you know the percentages.

BETH  I'm not blaming you, April.  I guess I just never thought it would happen to us.  I mean...I know lots of couples with straight kids, but...us? I just wasn't prepared.

APRIL   (*Goes to* BETH)   Look, Mom...Joan. I'm going away to college in a month. You won't have to worry anymore...

JOAN   Oh, honey, don't say that. We love you. We don't want you to go away.

APRIL   I love you too, Joan.

(*They all hug for a beat, then break - awkward again after this show of affection.*)

BETH   April?

APRIL   Yeah Mom?

BETH   (*Quickly*)   We have this friend...her name is Wanda. She's beautiful. Very sweet. She's pre-med. Why don't you just call her? What harm can it do?

APRIL   MOM - !

BETH   Just asking.

JOAN   Go run and change out of those icky clothes, dear. We'll all drive up to the cabin; spend the weekend together, eh?

BETH   Great idea darling!

APRIL   Uhm...

JOAN   What is it honey?

APRIL   I...I've got a date.

JOAN   *(Looks at* BETH)   I see.

BETH   *(Looking at floor)*   With whom?

APRIL   Mom, I -

BETH   *(Sternly)*   WITH WHOM?

APRIL   *(Barely audible)*   With Billy.

BETH   *(Swooning)*   Oh dear God.  It's too much.  Truly it is.
Joan - (*reaching out*).

*(*JOAN *moves to support* BETH *in her swoon).*

JOAN   *(She motions* APRIL)   It's okay, April.  She'll be fine.
We'll go to the cabin some other time, okay?

APRIL   *(With an appreciative smile)*   Okay, Joan.  Thanks.

JOAN   Sure honey.  *(Beat)*   I was straight once too, y'know.

*(Beth faints.  Lights down).*

**ANNE HARRIS (Playwright, Author, Composer) is the author of the
one-act plays IN THE GARDEN (Winner, 1984 Young Playwrights'
Festival) and COMING IN, and of two full-length plays - A
WOMAN'S PREROGATIVE and SCENES FROM THE PENITENTIARY
(Winner, 1993 Marc A. Klein Playwriting Award).  Her musical TOO
MUCH AIN'T ENOUGH has been performed in the regional theatres
and schools in upstate New York.  Ms. Harris is also the author of**

a screenplay entitled CUSTOMS, and has written short stories and children's tales. She is completing a Bachelor of Fine Arts degree at New York University's Dramatic Writing Program, partially funded by a 1993 Lee Stevens Scholarship and a 1993-94 Jean Stein Scholarship. Among her other accomplishments, Ms. Harris is the co-founder of LEND, INTERNATIONAL (Lesbian Exchange of New Drama), a non-profit presenting and resource organization for lesbian theatre arts. She has performed both original and popular music professionally, and is currently musical director of the Alternate Visions theatre troupe of the Youth Enrichment Services program at the New York Gay and Lesbian Community Center. A reader and a 'buddy' for the young Playwrights' Festival (a national play competition open to playwrights ages nineteen and under); she is a participant at the W.O.W. (Women's One World) Cafe in New York and supports PEN International. She lives in Brooklyn.

ANNE HARRIS

**"Out" to Play, original - 18x22 Oil on Rag Cotton by April A. Torres**

*"I didn't bring oil - I got your favorite,*
*Lanna Solei, in my orange bag."*
*- WHERE THE SEÑORITAS ARE*

# WHERE THE SEÑORITAS ARE *(excerpt of a full-length play)*
## by Janis Astor del Valle

*Music, "Voy A Romper", Tito Nieves.\* Scene One: Saturday morning, Memorial Day Weekend. Cherry Grove Beach, NY. Two women enter stage right and cross down center, begin setting up their blanket, etc.*

MAXIE  *(Looking in compact, applying make-up and constantly primping herself.)*  In the same breath, he's tellin' me, "I need my space, babe!" So I said, "You need your space? then vete par carajo and get your own apartment!" That boy has huevos *(motioning)*, I swear!  No digo yo, Luli, I been supporting him for six months, never asked him for a dime - never asked him for nothing - all I wanted was for him to help me carry the laundry, I wasn't asking him to help me do it!  "Why you gotta wait 'til the bottom of the ninth?  Mattingly is up, coño!" he yells from the living room and I'm halfway out to the car.  I mean, shit, I would love to watch the game, too, but things have to get done.  And he could've taped it!

LULI  Pendeja!

MAXIE  Que...

LULI  You're a pendeja, Maxie, letting these guys live with you, rent-free, cleaning up after them while they don't lift a finger around the house or anyplace.  Stretch out your side more.

MAXIE  Jorge worked!

\* **Written permission must be obtained from the recording company/artist to use this arrangement.**

83

LULI  (*Searching bags*)  Yeah, but you didn't see a dime of it, so what good is that?  Where'd you put the baby oil?

MAXIE  I didn't bring oil - I got your favorite, Lanna Solei, in my orange bag.

LULI  The gel or the creme?

MAXIE  The gel!

LULI  It's only number four sunblock!  (*Begins applying gel.*)

MAXIE  I don't need anything higher!

LULI  But I do!

MAXIE  Blanquita!

LULI  Don't rub it in!

MAXIE  You know, Benny works...sometimes.

LULI  Sometimes is right!  Two gigs in six months and that ain't no great shakes.  And what did he do with the money? Blew it on some blow.

MAXIE  He took me to the jai alai last week!

LULI  Super pendeja!  You don't even like the sport!

MAXIE  Why you always gotta' pick?

LULI  Maxie, mi hija, I'm not picking.  You told me yourself that Benny watches MTV round the clock.

*84*

MAXIE   It's part of his training, just like you train your body by watching Ailey or Martha Graham; well, Benny trains his instrument - his whole being - by watching MTV or VH1.

LULI   Yes, but I'm not spending every waking minute doing that!  I have a life"  If I'm not doing a show, I'm attempting to pay my bills -

MAXIE   Benny doesn't like attempting!

LULI   *(Under her breath)*  Benny doesn't like working, period!  *(She picks up an OUT Magazine and begins reading.)*

MAXIE   And what about Maria?

LULI   What about her?

MAXIE   What's she doin' with herself these days?

LULI   I don't know and I don't care!

MAXIE   You broke up again!  Ay, dio!  What was it this time?

LULI   Same ol' shit - she don't know what - or who - she wants.  *(Imitating)*  "Ay, baby, I'm so confused!  I love you and I love Raul!"

MAXIE   Poca verguenza! Pues, no more of this depressing talk.  We're here to have a good time!  You want me to do your back?

LULI   Yeah.

MAXIE   *(Spreading on gel)*   I'm so excited we're finally in Cherry Grove!  I can't believe I've lived in New York all my life and never once went to Fire Island! I didn't even know it was part of this state! *(Looking around. )* Luli, why are there so many women around?

LULI *(Absorbed in her magazine.)* Que que?

MAXIE Mira, Luli, there's no men in sight!

LULI There's some men over there.

MAXIE *(Searching)* Two! *(Staring)* Luli, they're gay men!

LULI No...

MAXIE Yes!

LULI And how would you know, Maxie?

MAXIE The guy in the pink Spandex bikini is massaging the guy in the Bugle Boy cutoffs - what's left of them - damn! Those shorts are so short, his cheeks are hanging out!

LULI Just like yours!

MAXIE Mine are not that short.

LULI Maxie, please! Your 505's are so short, I've seen a lot more than your cheeks!

MAXIE Stop! Anyway, it's different.

LULI How?

MAXIE If a guy's gonna' parade around like that, you know

he's a maricon!  Mira, what did I tell you?  The pink bikini's rubbing Bugle Boy's ass!

LULI   You're such a homophobe!

MAXIE   I am not!  I'm your best friend, ain't I?

LULI   So?

MAXIE   So - what are you trying to say?

LULI   Drop it, Maxie.   Mira, if you want to be around men, go to the Pines.

MAXIE   What's the Pines?

LULI   That's the beach where the boys are.

MAXIE   Well, then, let's go to the Pines!  I need some inspiration!  *(Starts to gather belongings.)*

LULI   I don't want to go to the Pines!  And I don't think you'll want to either.

MAXIE   Why not?

LULI   You're not their...type.

MAXIE   What, is it a racist beach?

LULI   No.

MAXIE   Then what?

LULI   The Pines is  mostly for...gay men.

MAXIE   Oh, that's just great!  Now we're forced to stay in
Cherry Grove, where the ratio is two gay men to every
*(realizing, looking around)* - Who is Cherry Grove for?

LULI   It's mixed.

MAXIE   Mixed what?  Gay men and lesbians?

LULI   There's some straights!

MAXIE   Donde?

LULI   *(Searching)*   Mira, there's a group!

MAXIE   A couple!  The only single people here are gay!  Luli,
when you invited me to Fire Island, you did not say the gay part
of it!

LULI   *(Sarcastically)*   Is there any other part?

MAXIE   You tricked me!

LULI   I did not!

MAXIE   You did, too!

LULI   I thought we were coming here to relax, not cruise!

MAXIE   Yeah, but -

LULI   But, what?  You're the one who said we hardly every
spend time together alone, that I don't make time for you, that

I'm always with Maria. So, here I am, setting aside my Saturday for you, my best friend of fourteen years and a half - almost fifteen - years and what do I get? *(Mocking)* Ay, Díos, it's a gay beach! Shit, I could have gone to Zulma's party in New Hope, but I chose to be with you!

MAXIE   And an island full of lesbians!

LULI   Por carajo!

MAXIE   *(Mocking)* I thought we came her to relax, not cruise!

LULI   What makes you think I'm here to cruise?

MAXIE   Luli, please, no soy estupida!

LULI   Maxie, whenever we go out, it's always to a straight place!

MAXIE   That's not true!

LULI   It is.

MAXIE   I went to the Cubby Hole with you!

LULI   Cubby Hole! Four years ago, just before it closed! We haven't been there since it reopened.

MAXIE   Well, I never really liked that place, it was always so dark and cramped and smoky!

LULI   There are other places, but you never bother to ask! You just take it for granted! We eat at straight restaurants, we dance in straight clubs, we go to straight movies -

MAXIE   I rented MAKING LOVE for you!

LULI   You never rented DESERT HEARTS!

*(Silence.)*

MAXIE   I just - I...it's really hard for me to look at two men together...and, two women is even worse...

LULI   Why?

MAXIE   I don't know, I just feel...uncomfortable around gay people...

LULI   But you don't feel that way around me...

MAXIE   As long as I don't picture you with another woman...

LULI   Well, damn, Maxie, I'm not asking you to picture anything, I'm just asking you to be my friend!

MAXIE   I am!

LULI   Not if you can't accept me for who I am!

MAXIE   I accept you, I just can't - the physical part...it grosses me out...

LULI   How would you feel if I said that the idea of you kissing Benny grosses me out?

MAXIE   It wouldn't surprise me; you never liked Benny.

LULI   That's besides the point!  What if I said that about you and any other man?

MAXIE   I guess I would be a little hurt, but I would understand because I know you're not into men.

LULI   So?

MAXIE   So I wouldn't expect you to like the idea of me kissing men.

LULI   Maxie, just because I'm not attracted to men doesn't mean I can't accept the fact that you are!  I don't care who you date, as long as you're happy.  But when I see these guys taking advantage of you and treating you like shit...I just think you deserve better.

MAXIE   And you think a woman would treat me better?

LULI   Not necessarily.  God knows I've had my share of losers.

MAXIE   You still lied to me by making me think this was a place for straights!

LULI   I didn't make you think anything!  It's a place for everybody, it just so happens that mostly gays come here.

MAXIE   That's what I mean, you lied!

LULI   I didn't lie, I just didn't tell you the details!

MAXIE   That's lying!

LULI   Maxie, I'm not gonna' argue with you!  You wanna' fight, put on your boxing gloves and go home to Benny!

*91*

*(MAXIE glares in hurt anger at LULI, then begins gathering her things.)*

LULI   *(Approaching)*  Maxie, I -

MAXIE   Dejame!

LULI   Please don't leave like this!  Let's -

MAXIE   You can keep the Lanna Solei, even though it is only number four!  Have a nice life!  *(She exits.)*

*(LULI stares after her a few moment, then lies face down on the blanket.  She picks up her walkman and rummages through her backpack, desperately searching for something.)*

LULI   *(To herself)*  Damn!  She's got my Tito Puente tapes!
*(Still searching her bag)*  And Santana!  Ay, caramba!

*(She puts on Linda Ronstadt's "Perfidia".\* As music swells, MAXIE re-enters.)*

MAXIE   Luli!

LULI   *(Turning around to see her)*  Maxie!  *(She rises to hug MAXIE)*  I'm sorry I said that about Benny!  I was just upset -

MAXIE   I know -

LULI   You got my tapes?

MAXIE   Yeah!  Mi hija, you've been my best friend since 9th grade.
\* Written permission must be obtained from the recording company/artist to use this arrangement.

LULI   Eighth!

MAXIE   Eighth - that's more than half our lives...so why'd you wait so long to tell me we never go to gay places?

LULI   I guess I was scared...

MAXIE   Of what?

LULI   I don't know...maybe that you wouldn't want to hang out if I spoke up.  I mean, Maxie, sometimes, you can be so homophobic.  It hurts.

MAXIE   I'm sorry,  mi hija.  It's just that, sometimes I get scared too.  Like even now, I can feel them cruisin' me, starin' me down with that look!

LULI   What look?

MAXIE   You know, that look - the way you look at women!

LULI   Please, don't be thinkin' everyone's after your ass!

MAXIE   They are.

LULI   No one on this beach is cruisin' you - trust me!

MAXIE   How do you know?

LULI   I know! *(Pause)*   How come you don't carry on like this when you think a guy's cruisin' you?

MAXIE   It's different...

LULI   How?

MAXIE   I don't know, it just is...

LULI   Is it?

MAXIE   Ay, Luli, you're making me all confused!  I don't wanna fight, I just want to spend the day with you, like we planned.  This is supposed to be our time together, remember?

LULI   Yeah.  I don't wanna' fight either.

MAXIE   I love you, Luli...

*(She hugs LULI.)*

MAXIE   Okay, don't hold me so long, people will think we're -

LULI   Ay, Maxie!  Get over yourself!  Where's my tapes?

MAXIE   In my backpack.

LULI   Can I have them, please?

MAXIE   You're going to listen to music now?

LULI   Yeah!

MAXIE   Oh.

LULI   What's wrong?

MAXIE   Nothing.

LULI   Maxie!

MAXIE   I just thought we were going to talk, that's all...

LULI   Okay, we'll talk.  What you wanna talk about?

MAXIE   Nothing!

LULI   *(Half to herself)*   What am I gonna' do with you?

MAXIE   Luli?

LULI   Yes, baby?

MAXIE   Do you love me?

LULI   Of course!

MAXIE   How come you didn't say it?

LULI   Maxie!

MAXIE   I told you I loved you...

LULI   I love you, Maxie.

MAXIE   More than Zulma?

LULI   Much more than Zulma.

MAXIE   More than Maria?

*(Silence)*.

MAXIE   Luli!

LULI   It's different!

MAXIE   Damn right!  You've known me more than half your life!  How long you known her?  Three months?

LULI   Four!

MAXIE   Hmmpphh!

LULI   Ay, muchachita, I love you, Maxie, more than Maria, more than Terricita, y Juanita, y Marisol, y Brooke -

MAXIE   Brooke?  Who the hell is Brooke?  You never told me about no Brooke!

LULI   Oohh, baby, I'll tell you about her now...

MAXIE   Ay, no, Luli, don't be gettin' too graphic, I can't handle that shit without my Cafe Bustelo!

LULI   I know!  That's why I packed a thermos, just for you!

MAXIE   You did?

LULI   I sure did   *(gets thermos out of bag)*   See, I'm always thinkin' of you.

MAXIE   I love you.  *(Pause)*.  More than Benny.

LULI   You better...

*(Lights fade.)*

# I'LL BE HOME
# PARA LA NAVIDAD

## by Janis Astor del Valle

*(Scene: 8:00 a.m., Christmas Eve in Mami's kitchen, Redding Ridge, Connecticut. Mami and Cookie are preparing dinner. Mami is marinating a roast pork and chopping garlic to mix with salt, pepper and oregano in a pilon - mortar and pestle. Cookie is peeling and slicing onions, green and red peppers)*

COOKIE   My friend and I went to El Fundador the other night, and, what a meal!  She had the arroz con pollo and they served it in this huge, cast iron pot - I mean, this thing was overflowing with mussels, shrimp, chicken and rice - but, you know, no beans.

MAMI   That's Spanish style - sin habicuelas.  Dame the salt.

COOKIE   How come you always make it with beans?

MAMI   Because that's Puerto Rican style.  Find a better knife, that one stinks.

COOKIE   It's not that bad.

MAMI   But it's taking you so long.  At this rate, we'll be eating Christmas dinner on Easter.

COOKIE   I just have to break every once in a while for my eyes.

MAMI   Here, let me do it!  You do the pilon.

COOKIE   No, it's Okay.

MAMI   Ay, pero look at your eyes!  C'mon, get away from there, I don't want tears in my sofrito.

*(They switch places.)*

COOKIE   Anyway, I had the pernil -

MAMI   Why did you have the pernil when I'm making it for tomorrow?

COOKIE   This was last week.  And, it was good, but not as tender as yours.

MAMI   Did they marinate it?

COOKIE   I didn't ask.

MAMI   It has to soak, like we did, overnight, in vinegar and a little bit of water.  Then, we cook it all day today.  They probably didn't let it soak and they probably didn't cook it long enough.  You have to be very careful with pork.  Especially if it's big - like this one - at least five to six hours.  And for the first hour or hour and a half, at 325.  Then, you can lower it.

COOKIE   Well, my friend tried their flan -

MAMI   Which friend is this?  The one you met at school?

COOKIE   Lena.  We met in dance class.  Neither of us -

MAMI   How do you spell it?

COOKIE    L - E - N - A!

MAMI    Oh, like Lena Horne.

COOKIE    Yes, except -

MAMI    That's a black name.

COOKIE    Ma! Anyhow, it's pronounced Ley-nuh! Short for Magdelena.

MAMI    Oh. She's Spanish?

COOKIE    Half - her mother's Dominicana, her father's black.

MAMI    He's a black Dominicano?

COOKIE    No, he's black - African American.

MAMI    What is your friend?

COOKIE    I just told you!

MAMI    No, I mean, is she...tu sabes?

COOKIE    What?

MAMI    Morena o negra?

COOKIE    She's about as dark as Titi Luisa.

MAMI    Your father's sister?

COOKIE    No, your sister.

MAMI    That's dark.

COOKIE    Mira, mami, don't start -

MAMI    Who's starting what?  I'm not starting nothing!  Where did you put the green peppers?  All I said was she must be pretty dark.

COOKIE    I can't believe you!  *(motioning)*    Over there, by the carrots.  Who were you engaged to before Daddy?

MAMI    Miguel Gonzalez.

COOKIE    And he passed for black.

MAMI    But he wasn't black.  His mother was Puertoriquena and his father was Dominicano - or was it the other way around?  Anyway, he was dark, but he wasn't black.

COOKIE    What's the difference?  We've got black blood in us - all Puerto Ricans do!

MAMI    We got a lot of things.  My mother was part Indian, too.

COOKIE    Native American.

MAMI    Whatever.  My grandfather used to call her Negrita.

COOKIE    Anyway...what was I saying?

MAMI    I don't know.  Something about your black friend.

COOKIE    No!  The flan!

MAMI  I never liked flan; I don't like anything that watery, makes me sick to my stomach.

COOKIE  Well, Lena and I split the flan. We were so stuffed by then. Lena said it was almost as good as her father's.

MAMI  Her father knows how to make flan?

COOKIE  Yeah.

MAMI  Her mother must have taught him.

COOKIE  No, actually he taught her. He was a cook in the Navy and stationed in Cuba before they got married.

MAMI  Oh, well, Cuban flan is different. Get me another green pepper.

COOKIE  Well, it tasted just like Tita's to me, and better than El Fundador's. *(Searching the fridge.)*  Where is it?

MAMI  The bottom drawer - left side, near the ajo. You tasted his flan?

COOKIE  Yes.

MAMI  When?

COOKIE  Thanksgiving.

MAMI  They invited you?

COOKIE  Yes. I told you before...

MAMI   You never said it was them.  You said a friend's.

COOKIE   Anyway, Lena's parents are in Santo Domingo for the holidays.

MAMI   That's nice.  It's beautiful this time of year.

COOKIE   Yeah.  She has no family in New York, not even the tri-state area.  Her nearest relative is in Texas.

MAMI   Ay, bendito, so far.

COOKIE   So, is it okay if she comes for Christmas -

MAMI   Ay, Cookie, I don't think your father will go for that.

COOKIE   Not to stay over, just for the day!

MAMI   He's never spoken to you about this - and he never will - but I know how he feels!  It's tearing him up!

COOKIE   How do you feel?

MAMI   Well, I have to agree with him.

COOKIE   Why?

MAMI   It's still very new to us.  All your life you like boys, and now, suddenly, a month ago, you tell us you're liking women?

COOKIE   There's nothing sudden about it.  I told you -

MAMI   I know what you told us.  I also know that just five

years ago you were ready to marry Jose!

COOKIE    Yeah, and marrying him or any other man would have been the biggest mistake of my life.  Mami, I've always been attracted to women - I just couldn't face it then -

MAMI    Please!  I don't want to talk about your problem!

COOKIE    Problem?

MAMI    Yes, that's what it is, a problem.

COOKIE    Why does it have to be a "problem"?  Why can't you just accept the fact -

MAMI    I don't have to accept anything!  You're my daughter and I will always love you, but I don't have to accept your lifestyle.

COOKIE    It's not a lifestyle, either!  People don't choose to be gay.  I didn't wake up one morning and say, 'Oh, I think I'll try a woman today!'

MAMI    You could've married Jose or the dozens of other men who chased you.  But you chose to ignore them.  That was your choice.

COOKIE    Yes, that was my choice, because I didn't love them. But I never chose to love, desire or have feelings for women. People can't decide things like that Mami!  It's just a natural -

MAMI    It's not natural!  A man and a woman together - that's natural!

COOKIE   Says Who?

MAMI   La Biblia.

COOKIE   La Biblia?  When was the first time you went to church?  1951, your wedding day, so don't give me that crap!

MAMI   Don't you curse at me!  I never let my sons swear in this house; I will certainly not let my daughter!

COOKIE   Crap isn't a swear word.

MAMI   The way you said it, it is.  And I don't like the tone of your voice you're using with me.

COOKIE   I'm sorry, but, Mami, it hurts when you say I've got a problem.

MAMI   I'm not trying to hurt you, I'm just telling you how I feel.  Homosexuality is not normal.

COOKIE   Did you decide to be heterosexual?

MAMI   Of course not!

COOKIE   Well?

MAMI   It's different!

COOKIE   How?

MAMI   I don't know, it just is!  That's the way it's always been and the way it should be.

COOKIE   Sounds like a Carly Simon song.

MAMI   What?

COOKIE   Nothing.  Mami...Lena is very special to me.  It's pretty serious -

MAMI   Yeah, they all were!  Special friends!

COOKIE   Ma!  That's not fair!

MAMI   Well, it's true!  All those women you brought here, over the years, making us believe they were just your friends - and your father and me took each one into our house like they were family -

COOKIE   They were!

MAMI   They were not!  Cookie, you lied to us!

COOKIE   I had to!

MAMI   You didn't have to do anything but tell us the truth.  At least then, maybe something could have been done...

COOKIE   Like what?  Electric shock treatments?

MAMI   I don't know...something!  We could have taken you to a doctor -

COOKIE   A doctor?  I'm not sick!

MAMI   Or a priest -

COOKIE   Most priests are gay themselves!

MAMI   Don't you speak about priests that way!

COOKIE   It's true!  At least, the ones I know...

MAMI   I will not have anymore of this ridiculous nonsense!

COOKIE   You want the truth?  I'll give you the truth:  I love Lena!

MAMI   And you loved the others and where did it get you?

COOKIE   This is different!  We've been together almost a year-

MAMI   Almost a year!  Big deal!

COOKIE   It is a big deal!  I'm in love with her!  We've talked about a future!  We're practically living -

MAMI   I don't want to discuss this!

COOKIE   Is that a "no" already or are you going to talk to Daddy?

MAMI   I will ask him, but I know my husband.

COOKIE   When are you going to talk to him?

MAMI   Don't push me Cookie!  I said I will talk to him!  I have to do it in my own time.

COOKIE   I know, but...Lena was going to catch the 9:45 out of Grand Central tomorrow morning...

MAMI   The 9:45?  To where?

COOKIE   Redding Ridge...

MAMI   Cookie, how could you?  How could you have invited her without asking first?

COOKIE   I never had to ask for Brian McAllister!  You went right up to him at Yolanda's wedding - never met him before that day - and invited him to spend the weekend with me in your home!  Without bothering to ask me, you asked him!

MAMI   Because I thought he was your boyfriend!  And he was a very nice boy.  And certainly the most handsome -

COOKIE   Well, he wasn't my boyfriend!

MAMI   But you brought him to the wedding!

COOKIE   It was a cover!  He was just a fuckin' cover date!

MAMI   Ay, Díos mio!  What did I tell you about cursing!  I have never heard the "f" word in this house and I'm not going to start now!  Not even your father has said that word to me!

COOKIE   I'm sorry for swearing.

MAMI   Who do you think you are that you can come into my house and use that kind of street language?  You may talk like that to your friends, but not to me!  I will not stand for it!

COOKIE   I said I was sorry.

MAMI   Put more ajo in there.

*107*

COOKIE   I'm finished.

MAMI   Did you put more ajo?  *(Looking over to Cookie.)*   I don't think you put enough.

COOKIE   It's more than enough, believe me.

MAMI   What time were you planning to go to the Mall?

COOKIE   I don't know...

MAMI   You better get a move on because they close early today.  The Mall is not gonna' stay open one minute past five because Cookie Mendoza is a last minute shopper.

COOKIE   It depends...

MAMI   On what?

COOKIE   How soon I get done here -

MAMI   Don't worry about that, I can finish by myself. Besides, we're almost done.

COOKIE   It also depends on what Daddy says about Lena...

MAMI   What do you mean?

COOKIE   I mean, I'm going to spend Christmas with  her. Whether it's here or New York.

MAMI   You're saying if Daddy says no Lena, you're going back to the City instead of spending Christmas Day with your family?

COOKIE   She is my family!

MAMI   I'm talking about your real family, your brothers and sister, your nieces and nephews - your mother and father, who brought you into this world -

COOKIE   Mami, why do you do this to me?  Why do you have to make me choose?

MAMI   Friends come and go, but your family will be there for you - always.

COOKIE   I know that.  But I'm telling you, Lena is more than my friend.  She's my lover, wife and partner for life.

MAMI   Wife?  Ay, no!  What are you telling me now?  That you're gonna' be the man?

COOKIE   Mami, no!  I love being a woman - it has nothing to do with that.  We're going to move in together and file for a domestic partnership.  Mayor Dinkins just passed this law -

MAMI   I always knew that city was crazy!

COOKIE   Maybe you think it's crazy, but Mayor Dinkins and thousands of others don't think so!

MAMI   Well, Mayor Dinkins and the thousands of others are not your parents.

COOKIE   You know, I been dying to ask you something...

MAMI   What?

COOKIE   Is Hector's girlfriend coming over tomorrow?

MAMI   Kathleen?  Of course, she'll be here.

COOKIE   And did Hector have to ask Daddy's permission?

MAMI   No -

COOKIE   I knew it!

MAMI   He's been going out with her for a while!

COOKIE   All of three weeks!

MAMI   He knew her from school!

COOKIE   I've known Lena a lot longer!  Mami, if you just give it a chance...

MAMI   It's not only me, it's your father, too!

COOKIE   You would all get along so well!  She's down to earth, very friendly, smart, warm, creative, a great dancer - she speaks Spanish fluently -

MAMI   Oye!  Are you telling your friends we only speak Spanish?  Just because I wasn't born in this country doesn't mean I can't speak English!  I can't spell too good, but I can speak English when I have to!

COOKIE   I know - she knows...mira, mami, she's a good person...I know Daddy would love her...she's a Yankee fan -

MAMI   Oh, that, he'll love -

COOKIE   And she plays the timbales - almost as good as Tito Puente!

MAMI   No one can play as good as Tito!

COOKIE   She's pretty close...

MAMI   Ay, Cookie...

COOKIE   Ay, Mami...remember when I was five and first started taking ballet?

MAMI   Yes...you used to cry everyday before it was time to go, you hated it so much!

COOKIE   I would get so tired holding onto that bar and listening to that boring music...I would do it because I kept thinking how much you wanted me to be the first Puero Rican in the Nutcracker...but, tu sabes, Mami, it wasn't in my heart...

MAMI   I know, mija...

COOKIE   But here I am, years later, all grown up now, and what am I doing?  I'm dancing.

MAMI   And starving.

COOKIE   I get by all right.  It's not ballet, but I'm still a dancer.  I've still had to work and train hard...but it's worth it to me, because I'm finally dancing all the dances I ever wanted to - merengue, jazz, salsa, mambo - all the dances that have always lived in my heart...remember when I finally told you I wanted to quit ballet and start taking modern?

*111*

MAMI   I cried.

COOKIE   At first...but, after the tears, came the love.  And the next day, you brought me to Miss Wilson's and signed me up for Modern Dance 10l.  You let me follow my heart, Mami.  That's all I'm asking you for now...

MAMI   Ay, mi hija...I don't wanna cry...

COOKIE   I know, but just remember what comes after the tears...(*Mami embraces Cookie*).

MAMI   Did I ever tell you you're a great dancer?

COOKIE   Great?  I don't think you ever used the word, great...good, maybe, but not great...

MAMI   Well, I think you're a great dancer!  Better than Chita Rivera!

COOKIE   Better than Chita?

MAMI   Yes.

COOKIE   How about Rita Moreno?

MAMI   Oh, si.  And you got better hair than both of them! Oye, can your friend bring the timbales?  Your father would love that...

COOKIE   Oh, I don't know...bein' she would be comin' by train.

MAMI   What train?  If we play our cards right, maybe you'll take Daddy's car and pick her up at her house.

COOKIE   Do you think I should...talk to him?

MAMI   Don't worry, you let me handle your father.

COOKIE   Thank you, Mami.

MAMI   Look at the time.   You better hurry, or they gonna' lock you in the Mall.  You laugh, but I heard that happened to someone last week.  Did you put more ajo?

COOKIE   Si.

MAMI   Put a little more.  A little ajo never hurt nobody.

COOKIE   Yeah, but we ain't got a little, we got a lot!  We gonna' have ajo comin' through our pores!

MAMI   That's all right; it's good for the soul.

*Wombyn's Hands   Photography by Ana R. Kissed*

◆◆◆◆◆◆◆◆◆◆◆◆◆◆◆◆◆◆◆◆◆◆◆◆◆◆◆◆◆◆◆◆◆◆◆◆◆◆◆◆◆◆

JANIS ASTOR DEL VALLE, Bronx-born 1963, second generation Puerto Rican, lesbian, writer, actor and director, is a 1993-1994 Van Lier Playwriting Fellow at Mabou Mines. At age seven, Janis was uprooted from her beloved Bronx barrio and transplanted amidst the cornstalks and whiskerwheat that was once New Milford, Ct. But on weekends, when she ventured back to the Bronx with her parents to visit their extended family, Janis often wrote and directed scenes in which she and her cousins performed at their Tita's (Grandmother's) house in Castle Hill. JACKIE, LEE AND CHICKY, was Janis' first play, written at age nine. Three years later she scripted THE FAMILY, which focused on the comings and goings of a dysfunctional, matriarchal family. Janis was sixteen before she wrote her next complete play, CHILD OF VISION, dealing with teenage alcohol and substance abuse in suburbia. In 1986, she returned to New York where she received a BA in Theater Arts from Marymount Manhattan College. Janis is a founding member of She Saw Rep, a lesbian feminist troupe which made its debut at the National Lesbian Conference, Atlanta. Co-founder of SOS (Sisters On Stage), a multi-cultural trio of lesbian theatre

professionals, she has performed her plays and poems in such spaces as W.O.W., the Duplex, Duality Playhouse, Madison Avenue Theatre and The Center. A stage reading of WHERE THE SENIORITAS ARE was held in Washington DC and Mabou Mines, and was performed two years ago with productions of the WOMEN'S PLAY-WRIGHT COLLECTIVE in NY. She dedicates her work to her lover ("Mi Estrella") and her family.

JANIS ASTOR DEL VALLE

114

# MAMI'S BALLET

by Janis Astor del Valle

tip
toe
Ing
A
Round, round the
Out
Skirts
Of
Your ambivalent heart,
I stop
to ask my heterosexual mother
what to do
about my non-committal lesbian lover

Look, ma,
No toe shoes
And I'm on point!

She loves me,
Loves me not ~
What do I do now, ma ~
Pirouette, pas do deux or
Stop?

Eye to Eye and
Ay!  to Ay! in

Puerto Rican Pride,
Mami and me,
We see
We smile
We meet.

"Merengue!" mami says.
So, I do.

# AFRICAN SEEDS
## by Janis Astor del Valle

He first mistook me for a WASP.

"They're African seeds,"
He tells me
With pride and sincerity
For a smile

"I made them myself -
You know African seeds?"
He asks, gently holding
A pair
Near, still
Smiling
Through the wind chill
Factor, twenty below
And counting
"Africa flows
In my Puerto Rican
Blood," I think while
Returning the smile
And almost whispering
My reply, "Yes, I
know African seeds."

But on the verge
Of my quivering lips
Lives
Another Truth -
Words that can
Not escape
The Prison of Fear;

In
Com

Plete
Sen
Ten
Ces
Born from
Over-Zealous thoughts -
Once Fallen on deaf ears -
Delivered, c-section

I had to cut, I had
To cut, I had to
Censor Myself
Although I know
Self-imposed silence
Is the worst kind
of noise,
I had to shut, I had
To shut, I had to
Lock the gate
To my cell, to my
Self, just
In case he also mis
Took me
For something else
When all I really wanted
To do
Was tell the brother
How
I know
African seeds
How
I have felt
Africa beating
In my lover's heart
How
My lover
Is

A Woman
An African-American
Woman

Woman
of color
of Soweto
of Sahara
of Kalahari
of Kawanza
of Fulani
of Mandela
of Malcolm
of King
of Niger
of Savanna
of Green
And Red
And Yellow
And Gold . . .

Beyond this pale
Olive skin, behind
These horn
Rimmed
Spectacles
Lives a Puerto Rican
Sister
Loving your earrings,
Brother,
Loving your African seeds
Loving them so much
But not loving my
Self enough
To tell you
They're not for me,
They're for my lover . . .

*Mexican Mother and Child*

*Photography by Lisa M. Wright*

118

*Photocollage by Sue McConnell-Celi*

**From the collection of children's mini-books, WOMEN WORKING, WHEN I GROW UP I CAN...**

*Photo by Andrea Weis*

SUE MCCONNELL-CELI                    Early  Spring 1990

# ON VELVET PAW
## by Sue McConnell-Celi

On velvet paw, she steals into my dreams
Agile, sleek, unannounced.
A break of a twig, a brush against the bush,
The earth barely detects the rustle of her leg
Before the storm of love lost.

We broke up not because of what we had,
But because of what could not have been ~

Senses stir within the private darkness, sleep.
The scent of her body, fragrant perfume
A fingertip away, I reach to touch the magic,
heart-shaped leaves and vines that shield her step,
In the tangled jungles of night
When the world is dead,
Softly, she comes.

Hold back the sun!
Delay the advance of harsh light, and Reality.
Let her tease me once more,
Rejoining, dabbling, tormenting,
Withdrawn, but not forgotten,
Though separated by countless people
   And daily chores,
Thousands, millions of breaths away,
Exists the whisper of ancient trees,
Now and then she speaks, ever gently, ever firm,
On velvet paw, she steals into my dreams.

ON VELVET PAW has appeared in NJ NETWORK Monthly Magazine and
WRITE FROM THE HEART (Author: Anita Pace; Baby Steps Press, 1992)

*Pot Luck Dinner (from lesbian images by ana r. kiss*

*"Honey, I know a lot of secrets...but this important - take
this down - if you never remember anything else...remember this.
I always assumed I had the right to any information, any truth, I want
If I didn't like what I found out, I learned not to take it personally.
This freedom of speech goes two ways...But I
also get to HEAR what I want, READ what I want...
It's time we gave each other the information we need."
~ SINS OF THE MOTHERS*

# SINS OF THE MOTHERS
## by Pamela S. Simones

DEDICATED TO THE MEMORY OF
EMMA JO MCCONNELL (1930-1990)
and
FLORENCE HENRY (1909-1991)

*Thanksgiving. An East coast apartment and a Midwest home.
But the stage need only show three areas, a bedroom, a kitchen,
and a back porch. The bedroom has a bed and a small table
near the bed with a hairbrush, a tape recorder, and a phone.
The porch has a telescope, adirondack chairs and a glider, if
possible. The kitchen needs only a counter with a coffee pot and
cookie tin and a table with two chairs.*

## CHARACTERS:

LEE LAMBERT - *Daughter of Joan, teacher of women's
history, working on an oral history project for her PhD.*

EMMA O'NEILL - *Lee's partner-in-life, established musician
and professor of music, warm, witty.*

JOAN LAMBERT - *Mother of Lee, model housewife and mother
who would be much happier if her eldest (Lee) were married.
Her clock stuck in the '50's.*

VIOLET UNDERGROUND - *Radical childhood friend of
Garnet. As avant garde as Garnet is conventional.*

GARNET HAYS LAMBERT - *Mother-in-law of Joan,
Grandmother of Lee, recovering from hip surgery.*

## SCENE ONE

*(Sound of flute playing THE ASH GROVE. Porch is in dim light. VIOLET is on porch looking at the constellations. JOAN is in the kitchen sweeping. LEE is in full light, sitting on her bed with a tape recorder.)*

LEE   Once upon a time... *(stops recorder.)*   Silly. *(Pause, shrugs.)*   Once upon a time there was a mother and daughter.  And they loved each other.  At least I THINK they did.  *(Brushes her hands through her hair.)*

*(JOAN stops sweeping, brushes back her hair.)*

LEE   Why do we choose to live with the people who aggravate us the most?  I remember...I remember a day when I was little.  Just me.  Mom was pregnant with Jenny.  I remember that because she didn't have much of a lap to sit on.  Dad was out of the town and it was just the two of us.  It was beautiful and warm and spring.  We went to the park and I ran and ran, laughing and tumbling and she laughed with me.  I put dandelions in her hair and she braided them in mine.  We had a picnic...*(Stops tape.)*

*(JOAN leaves.)*

LEE   I can't.  I don't know if this is real or just the way I would have liked it to be.  *(Starts tape.)*   When I was in junior high I was my most stubborn perfectionist self.  Everything I did had to be perfect, especially my art projects and I took great pains to do them just right.  But I was always behind.  Always near the deadline.  Twice my mother sent me off to bed and finished the project while I slept.  I was mortified, but what could I say?  My art teacher suspected something, I think.  She'd comment on how well I'd done UP TO A POINT. I finally learned not to tell Mom when a project was due. I worked on things at school, giving up my lunch hour to get them finished. I know she meant well but she was always finishing and fixing up things. In my space. *(Laugh)* Every time I moved she would descend on me ready to organize. I learned to put her in the kitchen and let her do all the work there. At least the rest of the place would look like me. When Emma and I moved into our new place together, she did the kitchen. And I freaked. It looked just like the way my mom would have done it. For days I was in a panic. Did I marry my mother? What had I done? Emma knew something was wrong. She played her music and waited. I broke down and told her she was just like my mother when she set up a kitchen. She looked at me kinda funny and said, "But Lee, I was just doing it the way YOUR kitchen had been." We laughed and made love and redid the kitchen to suit us TOGETHER.

LEE   I don't know why I can't laugh with my mother anymore. Sometimes I feel as if somewhere we got the myth wrong. She entered her own personal hell so I could roam the earth. And she stayed there. No matter how many messengers I send. She stays there.

*(Lights dim in the bedroom and come up on* VIOLET.*)*


## SCENE TWO

VIOLET   Ah, a lovely night to see the Pleiades, daughters of Aprodite, the seven doves. Some say the seven judges to the entrance to paradise. They'll cut out your heart and weigh it to see if you have loved well in your lifetime. The rending ones. Hail sisters, I know your names:  Alcyon, Electra, Merope, Maia,

*125*

Taygete, Celaeno, Sterope.  Do you know mine?  Violet Underground who searches the heavens.  Ah, Cassiopeia.  The mother who so boasted of her daughter's beauty, the gods grew angry and threw Andromeda in chains.  Rescued by Perseus.  Yes, there he is.  I wish I'd had a daughter to boast about.  All the things I've done in my life, yet I never had a child.  Not for want of trying, either.  Three, no four, husbands.  No children.  *(Pause)*  Now there's where I'd like to go next.  The Milky Way.  Wonder what kind of passport I'd need.  Silly old woman.  Time to get to bed with your notions.  *(Stands)*.  I'll get as close to the stars as I can.  Maybe I'll plan a tour of all the best observatories.  Yes.  There now.  I'll get there yet.  And I'll get Garnet out of her funk and take her, too.  We'll shoot for the moon, we will.  I wish...

*(*VIOLET *closes her eyes and wishes, then smiles and exits.)*

### SCENE THREE

*(Lights up on bedroom and kitchen.*  LEE *is sitting on the bed, talking on the phone.  In the kitchen,* JOAN *is talking on the phone and cleaning.  Sound of flute playing.)*

LEE   So is it all right if I bring Emma?

JOAN   I can't get over the fact that you're coming.

LEE   Well, you asked me.

JOAN   Did I tell you Mark Lewis got a divorce?  He'll be home for the holidays.

LEE   That's nice.  About Emma...

JOAN   She's most welcome, but you'll have to share a room.

LEE   We'll manage.

JOAN   His mother still has that prom picture of the two of you in her bedroom.  Says it was the nicest picture he ever took.  Is your hair short or long these days.

LEE   Short, Mom.  Ten years...

JOAN   I like it long.  When you were a little girl your hair was so long you could almost sit on it.  I'd brush it every night...

LEE   Mom...

JOAN   With you on my lap...

LEE   I looked like a dog...

JOAN   Such a sweet little girl.  You'll never guess what I found yesterday?

LEE   What did you find?

JOAN   Your first communion dress.

LEE   That's nice.  Just don't ask me if it still fits.

JOAN   Or if you're going to church?

LEE   *(Warningly)*   Mother...

JOAN   And I talked to Margaret Schilling the other day.

LEE   Really?  How's Sarah?

JOAN   She got married to a nice doctor in New Jersey.

LEE   Sarah MARRIED?

JOAN   I'm surprised you didn't know.

LEE   I knew she was in New Jersey.

JOAN   I got her new address from her mother so I could send a gift.  Honestly, Lee, I can't understand why you don't keep in touch with your old friends.  You and Sarah were so close, why I think you should have been one of the bride's maids, if not the maid of...

LEE   I'm really not into weddings.

JOAN   To think you didn't even know your closest friend...

LEE   I think you'll like Emma.

JOAN   You could bring your boyfriends.

LEE   It'll be just me and Emma.

JOAN   They could stay in Todd's room.

LEE   I'm not bringing any men.

JOAN   I can always make arrangements for your grandmother to be elsewhere.

LEE   I'm coming home to see Grandma.

*(JOAN cleans the countertop as she talks.)*

JOAN   I thought you were coming home to see me.

LEE   I am but...

JOAN   Of course, it's no surprise to me.  You finally come home for the holidays and it's because your grandmother broke her hip.  At least you didn't wait for her funeral.

LEE   Is Todd coming home?

JOAN   No.  He's going to celebrate with your father in California.

LEE   What's Dad doing in California?

JOAN   He has a business convention of some sort.

LEE   Why don't you fly out and join them?

JOAN   I can't leave your grandmother alone.

LEE   Emma and I would take care of her so you could go.

JOAN   I can't have strangers in the house while I'm not here.

LEE   Strangers?  I'm not a STRANGER.

*(Flute stops)*

JOAN   Emma is.

LEE   You won't have to count the silver.

JOAN   Don't be fresh with me, young lady.

LEE   Are you okay, Mom?  Is something wrong?

JOAN   Why should thee be anything wrong?  I'm just trying to plan Thanksgiving.

LEE   Well, it looks like there'll be me, Emma, you, Grandma. Four.

JOAN   Five.  Violet's coming.

LEE   You're kidding.  Really?  I love Violet.

JOAN   I never did like that woman.  She probably wants money from your grandmother.

LEE   I happen to think Violet's a scream.

(EMMA *enters the bedroom, mouths, "Your mother?"* LEE *nods "Yes".* EMMA *sits next to Lee and rubs her neck.)*

JOAN   You would.

LEE   Hey, she was a Bohemian before the word was coined.

JOAN   I hear she has a purple streak in her hair these days.

LEE   Is the rest henna red or her natural white?

JOAN   There is nothing natural about her hair.

LEE   You don't sound like you're in a happy holiday mood.

JOAN  Of course I am. You'll be here.  When can I expect you?

LEE  *(Turning to* EMMA *for confirmation)*  We'll be there sometime Wednesday afternoon.

JOAN  Fine.  If there are more than two of you, call me by Sunday.

LEE  It'll just be me and Emma, Mom.  *(*EMMA *stops rubbing* LEE'S *neck and kisses it.)*

JOAN  But in case you change your plans, call me by Sunday.

LEE  I'll call Sunday to confirm.

JOAN  I'll look forward to talking to you.

LEE  Bye, Mom.

JOAN  Aren't you going to say something else?

LEE  *(Looking at* EMMA*)*  I love you.

JOAN  I love you, too, sweetie.  Goodbye.

*(Both women hang up.  Lights down in kitchen.* LEE *pounds her chest.)*

LEE  Stabbed through the heart once again.

EMMA  Why do you do that to yourself?

LEE  Because I didn't give up anything for Lent.

EMMA   You have that look on your face.

LEE   What look?

EMMA   The one you had when I was introduced to you as MRS. O'Neill.

LEE   Oh, that look.

EMMA   *(Brushing* LEE'S *hair, soothing.)*   Lee...

LEE   *(Mimicking.)*   "Why didn't you tell me Sarah got married. I'm surprised you didn't know."

EMMA   I don't think she meant to hurt you.

LEE   'Course not.  She'll send Sarah a LOVELY gift.  Probably sign my name, too.

EMMA   Lee, all she knows is that you and Sarah were roommates.  Now, if Sarah had been a GEORGE...

LEE   If I had lived with GEORGE, she wouldn't be talking...

EMMA   Lee...

LEE   She's the founder of the no-sex-before-marriage club.

EMMA   LEE...

LEE   All right, all right.  Point taken.  Sometimes I think you like my mother more than I do.

EMMA   Tell me about Sarah.

*132*

LEE    You're changing the subject.

EMMA    No, I'm not.  So what did Sarah marry?

LEE    A DOCTOR.

EMMA    Did you tell your mother you married a doctor, too?

LEE    Did you hear an explosion in Cleveland?

EMMA    No.

LEE    Then I didn't tell her.  Emma...I am thinking about it.  It would be a good time to try because it would be just us, Mom, Gran and Violet.

EMMA    What about your father?

LEE    All of a sudden he and Todd are into male holiday bonding.

EMMA    What is your sister doing?

LEE    Jenny doesn't celebrate family holidays.

EMMA    Excuse me?

LEE    Her mother-in-law and my mother fought so much over whose turn it was to have THE CHILDREN that Jenny told them she'd not visit anybody on Thanksgiving, Easter, Christmas, or any day that Congress voted to give itself a long weekend.

EMMA    And they still talk to her?

LEE   She has their grandchildren.

EMMA   It's so fascinating discovering how your family celebrates the holidays.  So why don't they descend on her?

LEE   Have you ever seen a holiday fight over territorial rights to the kitchen?

EMMA   I bet I can top any one you've ever seen.

LEE   I remember a particularly nasty argument over giblets.

EMMA   I remember the time my family fought over temperature of the turkey.  I believe a knife was thrown by my father.  He divided the kitchen in half.

LEE   You rarely talk about your family.

EMMA   I don't talk about them at all.

(LEE *starts to say something.*  EMMA *raises her hand in warning.*)

EMMA   Don't push.

LEE   Families shouldn't be like that.

EMMA   Been working on your lectures about kinship and blood ties?

LEE  Biology does not a family make.  Love should make a family.  People should make their own little clusters.

EMMA   Family Clusters.  Sounds like a candy bar.

LEE   Let's cluster.

EMMA   *(Wrapping her arms around* LEE.)   Tell me a story.  I love it when you tell stories.

LEE   I knew it.  You just love my oral ability.

EMMA   Don't distract me.  I want a story.  I love to hear the way your voice changes rhythm when you tell a story.

LEE   You hear music and rhythm in everything.

EMMA   Tell me a story.

LEE   All right, all right.  When I was about thirteen, I read FRANNY AND ZOOEY.  I loved the book.  My mother thought it was too old for me.  Anyway, one of the things I liked best was the posterboard the older boys kept on the back of their bedroom door.  They wrote quotes from their favorite authors on it.  So, I decided to do that, too.  But Mom hated it.  Said it made the room look "jakey".

EMMA   *(Softly.)*  Jakey?

LEE   Jakey.  So she'd tear them down as soon as I put them up.  But I got her.  One day we got in a terrible fight.  It was our terrible fight for that week.  *(Wags her finger.)*  "I regret the day you were born."  I ran upstairs and wrote that on my poster.  She was hot on my heels.  "Just what do you think you're doing, young lady?" she said.  And I looked right at her and said - "Every time you say something nasty like that to me, I'm going to write it on this.  That way, I'll have a list of all the things I'll never say to my children."

*135*

EMMA   And you lived to tell this story?

LEE   Only because I took the poster down.  There was a colossal fight.  Jenny and Todd begged me not to argue with Mom and Dad because it made things harder for them, too.  To keep the peace I was a model child from that time on.  Did nothing offensive, said nothing offensive.

EMMA   Ever feel like an adopted child?

LEE   You mean I wasn't?

EMMA   We were both brought by the fairies.  *(Peering closely at* LEE*)*  Hurts, doesn't it?  Sarah.

*(*LEE *leans toward* EMMA *who folds her in her arms. Lights dim.)*


## SCENE FOUR

*(*JOAN *is in the kitchen.* GARNET *enters, using her walker.* JOAN *turns to see her.)*

JOAN   You shouldn't have come all the way down here.

GARNET   Talking to my granddaughter?

JOAN   *(Turning away)*   Yes.

GARNET   Going to be here for Thanksgiving?

JOAN   Yes.

GARNET *(Sitting at the table.)* Good.

JOAN   Would you like some coffee?

GARNET   Always do.   (JOAN *gets coffee for* GARNET.)   Any cookies?

JOAN   That's not a proper breakfast.

GARNET   I didn't live this long to start watching my weight.

JOAN   Hays ate the last of them yesterday.  I'll fix you a poached egg.

*(*GARNET *makes a face* JOAN *can't see.)*

GARNET   Do you still have some of those frozen waffles?

JOAN   You need your protein.

GARNET   I need waffles.

JOAN   There are only two left and they are for Hays' breakfast tomorrow morning before he flies out.

GARNET   Can't he pick some up on  his way home tonight?

JOAN   He'll be working late.  Your eggs will be ready soon.

GARNET   How's my granddaughter?

JOAN   Fine.  Won't bring home any boyfriends, though.

GARNET   Why does she need boyfriends?

*137*

JOAN   She needs to think about getting married.

GARNET   Plenty of time to think about it yet.

JOAN   When we were her age we were married and raising children.

GARNET   She's showed more sense than I did.

JOAN   (*Facing* GARNET)   She'll end up a lonely old maid.

GARNET   Honey, marriage doesn't protect you from loneliness.

(JOAN *backs down.*)

GARNET   I don't care if she never marries.

JOAN   As usual, I can't count on your help.

GARNET   Help what?  Get her married?

JOAN   Yes.

GARNET   If she wants to, she will.

JOAN   If you told her she should, she would.

GARNET   True enough.

JOAN   Always listened to you more than her own mother.

GARNET   True again.

JOAN   I never could fathom that.

GARNET  We always had an understanding.  Must be a carry over from a past life.

JOAN  That sounds like something Violet would say.

GARNET  Actually, I interested her in reincarnation.

JOAN  One life is enough for me.  How can you believe in that trash?

GARNET  I don't see any reason to disbelieve it.

JOAN  It makes everything seem so meaningless.

GARNET  I'd say just the opposite.

JOAN  Of course.

GARNET  Not too happy about Violet coming to visit, are you?

JOAN  She's your friend, therefore, she's welcome.

GARNET  Too bad Hays will miss seeing her.

JOAN  He has to do what's best for business.

GARNET  *(Turning)*  Those eggs ready yet?

JOAN  *(Turning away, checking)*  I forgot to turn the stove on.

*(JOAN begins to cry.)*

GARNET  *(Turning back)*  I'll get my own breakfast, honey.

(JOAN *rushes out.*)

GARNET *(Rising)* Wouldn't be you for all the world. *(Exits)*


## SCENE FIVE

*(EMMA is having a cup of coffee and doing a crossword puzzle on their porch. LEE enters.)*

LEE *(Looking over her shoulder)* Umu.

EMMA Oomoo? Are we learning a new language?

LEE *(Pointing)* Three-letter word for a Polynesian oven. U-M-U. Umu.

EMMA I thought you didn't like crosswords.

LEE You forget Killer Scrabble.

EMMA Ah yes, the great father/daughter battle of words. *(Looks up at LEE)* You have that look on your face again. You must have been talking to someone in your family.

LEE You mean you didn't hear me yelling?

EMMA Must have been your father. *(Rising)* Sit. I'll get you some coffee.

LEE A hug would be nice.

*(EMMA starts to hug LEE who backs away and begins pacing. EMMA patiently watches her.)*

LEE    I told him Mom seemed upset about Thanksgiving and his trip couldn't be THAT important that he couldn't delay a day maybe even see me for the first time in years and he kept making up stupid excuses and I said he made it look like he had some floozy stashed in California and he shouldn't be so damn obvious about it.  (Stops).   I know him.  He's cheating on her.

EMMA    So - do we pack the shotgun and some bandaids or forget it and go to the Bahamas instead of Ohio?

LEE    I convinced him to come home and bring Todd with him.

EMMA    Blackmail has its uses.

LEE    How DARE he - and at Thanksgiving.

EMMA    Maybe he loves her.

LEE    He's married.

EMMA    You thought I was married.

LEE    For one bleak moment.

EMMA    Would it have stopped you?

LEE    Dammit, Emma, that's not fair.

EMMA    Love isn't fair, Lee.  It strikes you when you least expect it.  And in order to keep it, you have to let it go.

LEE    You are talking in riddles.

EMMA    You know exactly what I mean.

LEE   So I'm supposed to give Dad my blessing?

EMMA   How about a little understanding?

LEE   They never gave me any.

EMMA   I know. But then they don't have your capacity for love.

LEE   Help me, Emma.  I don't know what to do.

EMMA   Nothing.

LEE   You mean don't tell my mother.

EMMA   I mean nothing.  You can't make everything all right. You can only make Lee all right.

LEE   Who invented this holiday anyway?

Mary & Me Coming together + letting go '92      Ana R. Kissed

**Photo by Ana R. Kissed**

*"Love isn't fair, Lee.   It strikes when you least expect it.*
*And in order to keep it, you have to let go."*
*~ SINS OF THE MOTHERS*

*142*

EMMA   A sadistic Puritan who had no music in his soul.

(LEE *starts to laugh.)*

Over the river and through the woods
To the Lamberts house we go.

LEE   Em, are you prepared to meet this family?

EMMA   Except for Jenny and the grandchildren.

LEE   They'll call.

EMMA   And we'll all talk at once on the extension.

LEE   There are only three phones.  We'll have to share.

EMMA   I don't have to talk to children on the phone, do I?

LEE   It would be significant if you did.

EMMA   There's nothing like taking your sweetheart home for
the holidays.

LEE   I must be crazy.

EMMA   Are you going to tell them about us?

LEE   I don't know.

EMMA   Then let's plan on enjoying ourselves.  I'll take my flute
and you take some tapes and your tape recorder.  I'll bet Violet
and Garnet have some good stories.  Not that they'll tell you.

LEE  *(Huffy)*  I'm responsible.  I'm mature.

EMMA  *(Faceoff)*  You still wear bunny slippers.

LEE  *(In her face)*  You got them for me.

EMMA  You're soooo sensitive.

LEE  You're soooo right.

EMMA  What time do we leave?

LEE  Whenever you're ready.  I want to stop at the store and get a case of frozen blueberry waffles first.

EMMA  Isn't your father allergic to blueberries?

LEE  Yes, but they're for Grandma.

EMMA  Woman, thy ways are devious.  *(Kisses her)*  But that's why I married you.


## SCENE SIX

*(Bedroom,* VIOLET *is brushing* GARNET's *hair.)*

GARNET  You still at that rape crisis center, picking uup radical notions?

VIOLET  You're changing the subject, Garnet.  So when are you going to move in with me?

GARNET  You don't want an old woman to take care of.

*144*

VIOLET   If you're that old, what does that make me, pray tell?

GARNET   I reckon that makes you old, too.

VIOLET   You're old as you feel.  That makes me 30.

GARNET   Makes me nigh a hundred.

VIOLET   Horsefeathers.

GARNET   *(Laughs)*   Long time since I heard that expression.

VIOLET   You'd hear a lot more familiar if you stayed with me.

GARNET   I belong with my family.

VIOLET   Where you're loved and cared for?

GARNET   I'm cared for.

VIOLET   But not loved.

GARNET   I don't hold that agin' her.

VIOLET   Why not go where you're loved?

GARNET   I don't want to be a burden.

VIOLET   So it's okay to burden Joan because she doesn't love you?

GARNET   *(Snaps)*   I didn't say that.

*(*VIOLET *fusses over* GARNET'S *hair.)*

*145*

VIOLET   A nice hint of electric blue would look wonderful.

GARNET   Goodness.

VIOLET   What's the problem?  Most women our age have pink or lavender hair.

GARNET   Violet, you are a caution.

VIOLET   Living with me would be a constant surprise.

GARNET   You low on funds again, honey?

VIOLET   For once, no.  My last husband set up a trust fund. I'd do better if you kept my books, but I'm not begging.  I want you to come live with me.

GARNET   Blood is thicker than water.

VIOLET   Don't you like being with me?

GARNET   Horsefeathers.

VIOLET   Then don't feed me that "blood is thicker than water" bull.

GARNET   Violet!

VIOLET   At least it's bull the way you mean it.  That phrase makes me think of something entirely different.

GARNET   And I'm about to hear it.

VIOLET   Blood is woman's tie.  Long ago women drew

together once a month to celebrate.

GARNET   And danced in a circle to ward off cramps.

VIOLET   Very likely.

GARNET   At least they didn't tell each other it was in their heads.  Violet, the things you make me say.

VIOLET   I do have a certain effect on people  So the blood tie is woman's tie and the water is semen.

GARNET   Do you eat with that mouth?

VIOLET   Let me see if I can get this right.  Once the conquering men took over, women's blood rites were considered unclean.  Women's bodies were a source of 'guilt and shame. They couldn't even go into the temple.

GARNET   Since when did you read the Old Testament?

VIOLET   Women were separated from each other and made to distrust each other because their source of strength was in the man who protected them.  If no man was around, they let their new faith protect them - God the father who gave birth to a son.

GARNET   Lawsy, Violet.  What HAVE you been reading?

VIOLET   Oh, lots of wonderful books.  It's amazing the things women can say and do these days.  Makes me want to live a long, long time juste to see where it will go.

GARNET   You should tell that theory to Lee.  Let her record it. Set back women's studies twenty years.

*147*

VIOLET  Why is that?

GARNET  We're not supposed to be radical.

VIOLET  We're SUPPOSED to be invisible.  Two old women.
But I'm proud to be an old crone.

GARNET  Me, too.

VIOLET  We are the wise ones.

GARNET  You tell them for me.  I stutter.

VIOLET  You have to learn to speak, too, Garnet.  The worst
thing that ever happened to women was the way were were kept
in line.  We were taught to be SILENT, we bore all our hurts
and wants ALONE.  We have mouthed half-truths from
generation to generation and have kept silent.  It's a sin, that's
what it is.  I don't know about the sins of the fathers but the sins
of the mothers is silence.

GARNET  I can't imagine my granddaughter would keep silent.
She's been a demon for truth ever since she was a little sprite.

VIOLET  She know everything about you?

GARNET  Doesn't need to, I'm her grandmother.

VIOLET  I love you, Garnet, so I'll tell you I'm sure she's got a
secret or two.

GARNET  Oh, I don't need to know everything about her.

VIOLET  Just what matters.

*148*

GARNET   What's gotten into you, Violet?

VIOLET   Oh, nothing.  Nothing.

GARNET   Well, I'm listening to your nothing and it sure sounds like something to me.

VIOLET   So, are you going to come live with me?

GARNET   You're changing the subject.

VIOLET   I know.

GARNET   I'll study it over.


## SCENE SEVEN

(JOAN *is in the kitchen.*  LEE *enters.*)

LEE   Hey, Mom.  Want some popcorn?

JOAN   No thanks.  You can enjoy it all.

LEE   Come on and join us on the back porch.

JOAN   Your father is due in any minute.  I want to make sure everything's done in here.

LEE   It's done, it's done.  Come on, it's a full moon and warm November.  If you dance naked in the full moon, you'll have good health for a year.

JOAN   More likely pneumonia.

*149*

*(*LEE *grabs* JOAN'S *hands and starts to swing her around.)*

LEE    Buffalo gal wontcha come out tonight
Wontcha come out tonight
Wontcha come out tonight
Buffalo gal wontcha come out tonight
And dance by the light of the moon.

JOAN    *(Resisting)*  I don't know WHERE you get your ideas.

LEE    What's life for if not to enjoy it?

JOAN    *(Letting go, dusting hands)*    Once you get married and
have children of your own, you'll know what life's all about.

LEE    I don't need a husband to make me a person.

JOAN    And what does that say about me?

LEE    It says nothing about you.  It says I'm not getting married.

JOAN    And just what do you mean by that?

LEE    *(Reaching for* JOAN'S *hands)*    Come out to the porch,
Momma.  Violet's teaching us the constellations.

JOAN    And I suppose you're recording it all for posterity.

LEE    You want to play the martyr?  Fine.  *(Backing away)*
Don't expect me to appreciate the sacrifice.

JOAN    I don't know what's gotten into you...You never talked
to me like this before.

LEE   Yes, I did.

JOAN   Is that what a PhD does for you?  Let's you insult your parents?

LEE   Not more than not having one allows you to insult your children.

JOAN   I don't care for any of your notions, young lady.

LEE   I'm no longer young.

JOAN   You're not old.

LEE   And I'm not a lady.

JOAN   I realize that.  Quit trying to shove it down my throat.

LEE   I don't want to argue with you.  I want you to join us on the back porch.

JOAN   I was never one for hen parties.  You go enjoy yourself.

LEE   Just once, tell me.  Why don't you like to be around other women?

JOAN   That's nonsense.

LEE   Oh really?  How many friends do you have, Mom?

JOAN   What a thing to say.

LEE   Why don't you like women?

*151*

JOAN   A woman is supposed to love a man, not other women.

LEE   That's not what I mean.

JOAN   Then what do you mean?

LEE   Why did you never like me?

*(Silence.* JOAN *turns her back on* LEE. LEE *exits to the porch.)*


## SCENE EIGHT

*(Bedroom.* EMMA *and* LEE *enter.* LEE *flops on the bed.* EMMA *sits next to her.)*

LEE   How do you like "The Family"?

EMMA   Is that what you call it?

LEE   Did Todd ask you out?

EMMA   Yes.

LEE   And?

EMMA   Is his hair really that blonde?

LEE   And?

EMMA   You've got a cuter butt.   What else do you want me to say?

LEE   I wondered what his technique is like.   Suave and

sophistocated, rough and ready, sensitive and needy.

EMMA   You want to know how he comes on to women?

LEE   I can't help it.  I changed his diapers.

EMMA   Your technique is MUCH better.  You should give him lessons. *(Coming on to her)*  Hey, so you're Lee's friend.  If you'd like to go for sushi, there's a little place called Chamberlain's near here.

LEE   And I know how you'd love to bite into raw fish.

EMMA   There's a reason why we live on the east coast.

LEE   And what is that?

EMMA   Because it's far, far away from the west coast.  He'll make some woman very unhappy.

LEE   He already has.

EMMA   Lee, this conversation really isn't about Todd, is it? *(*LEE *shrugs)*   Something is really bothering you, dear.  I know you.  It doesn't do any good to try to hide it.   *(*LEE *folds up into a ball)*
Buffalo gals wontcha come out tonight
Wontcha come out tonight

LEE   *(Moaning)*   This buffalo gal **can't** can't come out.

EMMA   *(Putting her arms around Lee)*
Oh she danced with the girl with the hole in her stockin
and her knees kept a rockin, and her toes kept a knockin

*153*

LEE   Did you hear me?   *(Emma nuzzles her).*   And don't lick my ear!

EMMA   Tell me a story.

LEE   Sing me a song.

EMMA   I'm the guest in this house.   Amuse me.   Besides, if I sing to you, you'll continue to obsess about your family.   Tell me a story.   Tell me your FAVORITE story.   I'll give you a kiss if you do.

LEE   Well......I remember when I first noticed you.

EMMA   And when was that?

LEE   You know this story.

EMMA   Tell me.   It's my favorite.

LEE   It was your first faculty recital.   You played a composition you had written.

EMMA   Toccata and clam sauce.

LEE   At the reception you got smashed on champagne.

EMMA   *(Flourishing)*   My trilogy will be the three stages of a woman's life - Premenstrual, menstrual, and post menstrual.   And it will be known as -

EMMA AND LEE   The Menstrual Cycle

LEE   I thought you were nuts.

EMMA   Thanks.

LEE   Have to be to put up with me.

EMMA   Pity poor Lee.   I love you anyway.

LEE   Why me?

EMMA   You are a great "straight man".

LEE   Me?  You think I can play Ethel to your Lucy, Shirley to your Laverne?

EMMA   Sodom to my Gomorrah.

LEE   *(Grabbing her.)*   Sodom at your service.

EMMA   Have you forgotten where we are?

LEE   Yes.

EMMA   Good.  Let your mother go, Lee.  Give her what she will accept, but let her go.  Enjoy your work, our love, and life.  Go in search of your stories.


## SCENE NINE

*(*VIOLET *is sitting on the porch.*  LEE *comes out to talk to her.)*

LEE   Gran okay?

VIOLET   She's fine.  Just tired.  Where's Emma?

*155*

LEE   She'll be here in a minute.  A November night like this is hard to come by.

VIOLET   Mind if I sit here a spell?

LEE   We'd love it.   (VIOLET *takes her hand.*)

VIOLET   I was trying to remember the last time we saw each other.

LEE   My graduation?

VIOLET   I don't think it was that long ago...

LEE   There may have been a holiday.

VIOLET   Easter.  It was Easter.

LEE   Gran's birthday.  I brought the chocolate; you brought the champagne.

VIOLET   I wish you'd had your tape recorder going that day.  I seem to recall we were memorable.

LEE   Actually, I went home and wrote down as much as I could remember.  Now that you mention it, I think that day may have been the start of my interest in oral history.

VIOLET   It's nice to know we're been a good influence.

LEE   The best.

VIOLET   Then why don't you visit more often?

LEE   I've been to see Gran when you weren't there.

VIOLET   Not as often as you might.

LEE   Well, I...

VIOLET   I know how life is.  You get busy and you think you'll always have the chance to do something.

LEE   Is she ill and not telling me?

VIOLET   She's a tough old bird like me, but nobody lives forever.

LEE   I can't imagine being without her.

VIOLET   All the more reason to visit her while she's alive.  If you only realized how much it means to her.  She talks for days before you come and dotes on the memory of it for weeks.

LEE   *(Stammering)*   I...I can't promise.

VIOLET   Emma wouldn't mind.  She seems to like Garnet. *(*LEE *stares at* VIOLET.*)*   Emma is your lover, isn't she?

LEE   Boy, you don't pull any punches, do you?

VIOLET   I think Emma is wonderful.  You shouldn't use her as an excuse not to visit your family.

LEE   I'll visit Gran.  I promise.  But I can't take more than two days of my mother.

VIOLET   That's 24 more hours than I can take.  Poor woman.

I feel sorry for her. I asked Garnet to come stay with me.

LEE    Really?

VIOLET    I can take care of her.

LEE    I don't doubt that. Is she going to do it?

VIOLET    I think she's afraid of what the family will say.

LEE    I can't imagine Gran being afraid of anything.

VIOLET    Any good word you could put in for me...

LEE    I'd be happy to.

VIOLET    And I think you ought to tell her about you and Emma. I'd like your Grandmother to know you are with someone who loves you. She won't worry about you so.

LEE    She worries about me?

(EMMA *comes out on the porch.*)

EMMA    See any falling stars?

VIOLET    I'll go see about Garnet.    *(Violet exits.)*

EMMA    *(Sitting next to* LEE, *helping her with her jacket)*  You look like hell.

LEE    Violet reminds me of a game show hostess who gets people to admit things they'd never tell a single soul - and they end up broadcasting it on prime time.

EMMA   She knows we're lesbians.

LEE   She wants me to tell Gran about us.

EMMA   Are you going to?

LEE   I couldn't stand to lose her good opinion.

EMMA   Lee, she LOVES you.  I can see that.

LEE   That's  no protection.

EMMA   Protection.  Protection from what?  Your grandmother never wanting to see you again?  I can't see that happening.

LEE   But what if she never wants to discuss it again?

EMMA   You're not discussing it now.

LEE   Is it obvious I'm avoiding something?

EMMA   Maybe I'm just too sensitive.

LEE   Do you feel I ignore your existence?

EMMA   No, love.  I can tell when you're holding back something.  Aren't the stars beautiful tonight?

LEE   *(Pointing)*  Cassiopeia.

EMMA   *(Drapes her arm over* LEE'S *shoulder, looks up at the sky and softly begins to sing)*
Tell me why the stars do shine
Tell me why the ivy twine

Tell me why the sky's so blue
And I will tell you
Because God made the stars to shine
Because God made the ivy twine
Because God made the sky so blue
Because God made you
That's why I love you.

*(JOAN listens from kitchen. GARNET and VIOLET sing from bedroom. Lights down on porch. Lights down in bedroom.)*

JOAN    That's why I love you.
*(Goes to entrance to kitchen)*    Hays, do you want more coffee?
*(Pause)*    The pie's for tomorrow and you know it *(laughs)*.    No, you can't twist my arm.    Pie won't be cut until tomorrow.
*(JOAN sits at table and turns the tape recorder on.)*

JOAN    I don't see why anyone would be interested in something I would say, but I'll do it to help out with your project.    I'll tell you a little about your grandfather:    I was born December 7.    After 1941 my birthday was never celebrated on that day, because my oldest brother had been stationed at Pearl Harbor.    Daddy would go off by himself; never would say where he went.    But he made it up to me.    He always made it up to me.    It couldn't have been easy trying to be both mother and father to me, not only the youngest but the only girl in the house.    I don't know how he did it, but I always felt special.    Daddy would carry me on his shoulders...*(JOAN gets choked up, stops the recorder)*    I don't need this grief *(VIOLET begins singing.)*

VIOLET    Lavender blue diddle, lavender green
When you are queen diddle diddle
I shall be king...*(continues song...)*

JOAN  *(JOAN Turns recorder back on)*   I got married right out
of high school.  Hays was quite handsome then.  All the girls
were jealous.  An older man.  He was a go-getter, wanted to
make his mark.  Right after the wedding, he whisked me off to
Iowa.  Fields and fields of corn.  He was an engineer, but he
wanted to live on a farm.  So we lived in the country, five miles
from the nearest farmhouse, fifteen miles from the nearest city.
I didn't know how to drive.  I got pregnant.  Hundreds of miles
away from my Daddy.  I wanted to call him...Take me back,
Daddy.  Please I 'm so lonely.  I don't know this man.  I'm so
unhappy.  But I was going to have a baby - Lee.  I named her
for Miss America.  I couldn't run away from my responsibilities.
Daddy wouldn't have understood it.  He wouldn't want me to be
so unhappy, but he wouldn't understand.  He and Mom had been
married for twenty years - no problems.  I hadn't even given
Hays six months.  I didn't want to disappoint Daddy.  I wanted
him to always love me and be proud of me.  You can't love a
child if you're not proud of her.  *(JOAN stops the recorder
horrified by what she has said.  JOAN ejects the tape, looks at it,
puts it into her pocket.  JOAN checks to make sure kitchen is
neat, turns out light.)*


**SCENE TEN**

*(LEE and EMMA rush into the bedroom.)*

LEE  My favorite blouse.

EMMA  *(Unbuttons the blouse)* Hurry and take it off.  I'll rinse
it out.

LEE  I can do that.  *(Takes off blouse, puts on t-shirt.  EMMA
gets tape recorder, exchanges it for the blouse.)*

*161*

EMMA  No.  Here.

LEE  What?

EMMA  You record.  You speak into the microphone and recount the day you stood up to your parents.

LEE  This is silly.

EMMA  You just press these two buttons and talk.  *(Exits with blouse.)*

LEE  This really is...*(presses two buttons)*  Thanksgiving, 1987. Today.  The day I stood up to my parents.  Well.  We, my mother and I, were starting to put the food on the table when I realized there were only six places set.  Dad, Todd, Mom, Emma, me, Violet.  But not one for Grandma.  I thought it was an oversight.  Dad started carving the turkey.  Mom was fixing the gravy.  So I got an extra place setting.  But - oh, no - Grandma's arthritis is acting up.  She can hardly handle a fork.  I said I'd feed her.  Dad said, "Nonsense."  Mom said she didn't want her best linen ruined.  I took the gravy boat and poured it down my favorite blouse.  "There.  I made the first mess.  I've spilled it everywhere.  Are you two embarrassed to let me sit at the table?  Shall I eat in the garage?"  Mom started crying.  Dad started ranting.  I said, "If we are to be a family, we must not have more pride for ourselves than love for each other.  Home is the place where one is supposed to feel secure.  Home is safe harbor, not ridicule and rejection.  This is Thanksgiving, for Pete's sake.  Can't we accept each other as human being even ONE day a year?"  My mother stopped crying.  My father shut up.  Todd sneered a little.  Emma rushed me up to our room to change, afraid the gravy would burn me.  They're setting a place for Grandma.  Violet will help her. *(LEE stops recorder, pats it.)*

## SCENE ELEVEN

(EMMA *is playing her flute in the bedroom.* LEE *is taping* GARNET *and* VIOLET *on the porch.* JOAN *is in the kitchen getting dessert for the boys.*)

JOAN   *(At doorway to kitchen.)*   You boys ready for another piece of pie?   *(Laughs, pleased.)*   I swear, bottomless pits.

GARNET   *(To* LEE*)*   I hear you had fire in your eyes today.

VIOLET   Now I wonder where she got that temper.

GARNET   Comes by it honest.

LEE   May I tape this?

(VIOLET *looks to* GARNET.*)*

GARNET   Go right ahead, honey.   Anything we can do to further the cause of science.

VIOLET   Garnet, you are a caution.

GARNER   Horsefeathers.   That the kind of talk you want?

LEE   You're teasing me. And what do you mean by my temper?

VIOLET   Why, Garnet, of course.

LEE   Grandma?

(JOAN *exits with two pieces of pie, returns, gets two cups of coffee, exits returns.*)

GARNET   You missed out on the best years.

VIOLET   Which ones were those?

GARNET   First years of my marriage.

VIOLET   Oh, my.

LEE   You and Grandpa fought?

GARNET   Honey, he came to be a good man, but we had a rough row to hoe for a few years.

VIOLET   That's a nice way to put it. Poor old Eddy didn't know what he was getting into when he married you.

GARNET   Your Grandpa was out of work in the early '30's.

VIOLET   Never ran out on you.

GARNET   That's right. Lots of men did. Left their little babies, took to the rails. Eddy started drinking after he lost his job at the mill. And he went for it in a big way. Until I put a stop to it. One night he got home about three in the morning. He was making the awfullest racket. Couldn't fit his key into the keyhole.

VIOLET   He was blind drunk.

GARNET   I said, "Vi, bring me some water." Vi was staying with us then.

VIOLET   Tell the truth. My husband was in jail for bootlegging.

*164*

GARNET   Your EX-husband.  And I didn't want Eddy to end up like him.  So Vi boiled the water...Eddy was still outside slumped against the door.  I leaned through the transom and poured it on him.  Scalded him something fierce.  "You dare come home like that agin and it'll be pork grease next time!"  Never saw a fella sober up so fast.  He went out looking for a job next day.  Ended up moving to Akron to work for the rubber industry.  But he said a word about what I did.  Never came home drunk again, neither.  Man needs a good dose of reality now and then.

LEE   Tell me about it.

GARNET   Stop that thing for a minute.  (LEE *stops recorder*)  Your daddy fooling around with someone?

LEE   Grandma, he's your son.

GARNET   Been acting like a man with a mission.  I know when Hays is up to no good.  This business about being in California for Thanksgiving.

LEE   Obvious, wasn't it?

GARNET   Not to your mother.

VIOLET   Is anything obvious to her?  I think she constantly lives in a dream world.

LEE   She always believes in happy endings and won't read a book that doesn't end that way.  Always expects the best, except where I'm concerned.

GARNET   Never did understand that.

VIOLET   She's jealous.

LEE   Of her own daughter?

VIOLET   You're her first born.  She expected you to put her first in everything.  She was to be the center of your universe.  Only, I gather, you were perverse and wanted to be your own person rather than a carbon copy of one of her happy endings.  And you dote on your grandmother rather than her.

LEE   I can't live her life for her.

VIOLET   She doesn't realize that.  All she knows is that you WON'T live her life for her.

LEE   Will you tell me about home?

GARNET   Go ahead, turn it on.

VIOLET   We had a lot of fun growing up in Hanging Rock.  It was long and narrow in those days, before the highway cut it in half.  I reckon it was five miles from one end to the other.

GARNET   Everybody knew your business.

VIOLET   True.

GARNET   And we may have been small, but we had us some colorful characters.

VIOLET   Doc Creighton.

GARNET   Now there was a piece of work.

LEE   I don't remember a Doc Creighton.

GARNET   He died long before you were born.

VIOLET   They said he was the meanest man there ever was.
Someone heard this, I don't know whether my Dad told me or
what. There was a druggist who'd borrowed money from Doc
Creighton to buy a house. Come close to the last payment and
the druggist couldn't come up with all the money. Been right on
time all along, but Doc took it from him. All legal, of course.
Druggist - what was his name - hung himself. Old Doc - well,
he was murdered soon after - chloroform. And here's the funny
part. Well, it isn't funny. His wife had died before he did and
he'd ordered a casket from across the river. They went to all
sorts of trouble to get it and when it came in, he said he didn't
want it. When he died they stuck him in that casket. But his
belly was so big, they had to remove his intestines to fit him in
it. They buried THEM in the backyard of the funeral parlor.
They didn't know at the time that he'd been murdered. Course,
when they figured that out, the undertaker had to admit what
he'd done. It had to be dug up to be tested for chloroform.
Liked to ruin him, it did. They'd had such a good family
business and it really set them back for a couple of years.
Remember that?

GARNET   *(Dryly)*   It was before my time.

VIOLET   Now you tell a story, Garnet.

GARNET   I don't tell them as well as you do.

VIOLET   Come on.

GARNET   Let's see. Now who was - who was that doctor who

brought me into the world. *(GARNET now looks to VIOLET.)*

GARNET and VIOLET   Doctor Thomas Gray.

GARNET   That's right.  His daddy built Gray Gables, a
beautiful mansion at one end of Hanging Rock.  Jimmie Klutz...

LEE   KLUTZ?

GARNET   Yessir, Jimmy Klutz bought it.  My daddy was his
gardener.  That's how I came to be a good gardener.  He'd break
off a little piece and bring it home and say, "Here, Garnet, it'll
grow for you."...Now what was it he made his money in?

VIOLET   Banking, banking.

GARNET   I believe he was a banker.  A friend of mine, Vinnie
Wilson, worked at Gray Gables as a maid and she wanted off
and asked me if I'd like to work there.  So I did.  Worked pretty
good there till the first Sunday.  They had chicken for dinner and
the cook asked me what piece I liked best.  I said, "Drumstick."
So she put one back for me.  But Mrs. Klutz noticed there was
one drumstick less and she came into the kitchen.  Told the cook
that ALL the food had to be served to them first and we could
have what was left.  I said, "No, thank you.  I don't eat what
somebody has picked over."  So I quit right then and there and
went home.  I used to like the drumstick, but I never ate another.

VIOLET   See, I told you about her temper.  Quit over a
drumstick.

GARNET   I calmed down.  I got married and calmed down.

VIOLET   Eddy might take exception to that.

*168*

GARNET  God rest his soul.

VIOLET  I remember the first time I met him.

GARNET  Square dance.

VIOLET  At Pop Gilbert's.  He couldn't take his eyes off you.

GARNET  Danced all night and when it came time to go home there was a big mud puddle.  He picked me up and carried me over it.  And that was that.

LEE  You sound like you're wearing down a bit.

GARNET  All this talking.

VIOLET  We can do some more tomorrow.  And when you come to my croning party we'll make a videotape.

LEE  Croning party?

VIOLET  I figured you'd know all about things like that.

GARNET  She tried to explain it to me, too.

VIOLET  I went to one when I visited California this past June.

LEE  Is this a new West coast fad?

VIOLET  Shame on you.  Some good CAN come from California.

GARNET  Like your favorites Reagan and Nixon.

LEE   Grandma, please.

VIOLET   Lynn Andrews, Judy Grahn, and Starhawk.

LEE   I stand corrected.

GARNET   Explain to me what a crone is again.

LEE   It's one of the three aspects of the goddess.

VIOLET   And of all women.

LEE   The virgin, the mother, the crone.  The crone is the wise woman.

VIOLET   And a croning party is a rite of passage to celebrate the third phase of a woman's life.  Most women have it on their fiftieth birthday.  So I'm old enough.  I want to officially become a crone.

GARNET   And be known for your WISDOM?

VIOLET   I've been known for everything else.

GARNET   That's for certain sure.

(EMMA *stops playing flute.*)

VIOLET   Shoot, she stopped.

GARNET   I was hoping she'd play me to sleep.

LEE   I'll ask her to.

GARNET   Don't bother her.

LEE   She'd love it.

VIOLET   Do you think she'd play for my party?

LEE   Ask her now so she can plan for it.

VIOLET   I'll have a Professor playing at my party.

GARNET   Whoooeeee.  Ritzy.  We don't do so bad for two old ladies, do we?

LEE   You don't do bad at all.

(LEE *helps* GARNET *exit.  Lights down.*)


## SCENE TWELVE

(EMMA *is in the bedroom.*  JOAN *knocks on the door.*)

EMMA   Come in.

JOAN   I hate to disturb you.  The music's so lovely.

EMMA   Thank you.

JOAN   It must be wonderful to make such nice music.

EMMA   It is.  Would you like to sit?

JOAN   No, no. *(Sitting on bed)* I just wanted to ask you something.

(EMMA *begins putting her flute away.* JOAN *doesn't say anything. After some silence* EMMA *looks up.)*

EMMA   How may I help you?

JOAN   I want to thank you for restoring the peace today.  I don't know what got into Lee.

EMMA   *(Busying herself)*  And?

JOAN   And she needs to think about getting married.

EMMA   Shouldn't you be talking to her about this?

JOAN   She won't listen to me.  And her grandmother won't tell her either.

EMMA   You want me to talk to her?

JOAN   Would you?

EMMA   Why is it so important that she be married.  Aren't you proud of Lee?

JOAN   Hays and I are proud of all our children.

EMMA   Do you think that if she were married, she'd be more like you, that you could understand her then?

JOAN   Yes, that's it.

EMMA   Did you find it easier to talk to your mother after you got married?

JOAN   My mother was dead long before I got married.

EMMA   I'm sorry.

JOAN   You were married, weren't you?

EMMA   Yes, for a blessedly short time and I never will forgive my mother for what happened.

JOAN   She must have done something terrible.

EMMA   She testified for my husband in the divorce suit.

JOAN   Your own mother?

EMMA   I don't talk about it.

JOAN   I understand. I would be proud if you were my daughter.

EMMA   I wish you and Lee got along better.

JOAN   You think I argue with my daughter all the time? Is that what she'd led you to believe?

EMMA   I wouldn't call it arguing. You seem to just miss connecting with each other.

JOAN   My daughter has never been willing to meet me halfway.

EMMA   She can be stubborn.

JOAN   Always was, even as a child. There was a part of her I never could control or understand. I always knew it would put us at odds with each other. I just can't believe she's the same little girl who used to bring me dandelion bouquets. And I'm beginning to wonder...is Lee - you know, doesn't she LIKE men?

EMMA   Are you asking me if Lee is a lesbian?

JOAN   I hate that word.

EMMA   I think that is something you should ask Lee.

JOAN   You were married. You know better.

EMMA   That's true.

JOAN   *(Patting her)*   I know that the right man will come come along for you.

EMMA   I am certain I can find the perfect mate.

JOAN   Watch out for Lee.

EMMA   I'll consider it a personal responsibility.

JOAN   *(Smiling)* You make me feel better. *(Rising)* Going to play some more? I love to hear the flute.

EMMA   Maybe later. What's your favorite song?

JOAN   *(Shy)* Oh, I like almost anything. Thank you for asking.

EMMA   You're welcome, Mrs. Lambert.

JOAN   Joan.

EMMA You're welcome, Joan. *(JOAN exits, EMMA shakes head.)*

*174*

## SCENE THIRTEEN

(VIOLET *is sitting on the porch steps, holding the recorder.*)

VIOLET  A recording for Lee. My favorite memory. My favorite memory is my favorite person, a golden girl who took my breath away at first sight. I told her jokes, made her laugh, acted the fool, sneaked her foods her parents wouldn't let her have - chocolate, candied oranges, anything sweet. I was seven years old when I met her. My family was wild and rough and tumble. Hers was strict and proper. I daresay neither family had much money, but we sure had more fun with ours. Her parents didn't seem to mind me and I was on my best behavior around them so they'd let me visit. I loved being near her. She didn't have to say a think or even acknowledge me. But she did. We shared our darkest secrets and our brightest hopes. She'd let me make up all kinds of silly daydreams, encourage them even, and never laugh at my ideas. The wilder, the better. She said I had to reach for the moon for her as well as for myself because she was too afraid to try. And so I did. And failed more often than not. But she'd bail me out, dust me off, fill my purse, and send me on my next adventure. "Make it a real juicy one this time, Vi." She was named for a jewel, Garnet. And I have always preferred garnets to rubies, emeralds, even diamonds. I have fought for everything from gay rights to gray rights. I've travelled to thirty countries. I counted one time. Kept all my passports to prove it. I've had three husbands - no, four, artistic triumphs, nights in jail. But always my center, my beacon was Garnet. If she said, "Go to it," I had no fear. She's the one who named me Violet Underground. Said to her it meant that I could bring forth beauty even in the darkest hole. That was back - well, a long time ago. But you'll have to ask your grandmother about that.

*(EMMA appears. VIOLET stops the tape.)*

VIOLET   She talking to her grandma?

EMMA   Yes.

VIOLET   You a little worried?

EMMA   Every quest for truth is fraught with peril, but she wants nothing less. It's one of her qualities I most admire.

VIOLET   She sure knows how to get a body thinking. I guess I've been quite a colorful character.

EMMA   Well, if your hair is any indication...

VIOLET   You two'll have to come for a weekend and I'll get out all my scrapbooks and tell you about Prohibition, union fights, and all my friends at the follies.

EMMA   The Ziegfeld follies?

VIOLET   I did some theater in my time. *(Elbowing EMMA)* A chorine.

EMMA   Violet, you are full of surprises.

VIOLET   Fuller than you think. I'm going to have me a croning party real soon. Maybe when Garnet moves in with me, we'll celebrate.

EMMA   Sounds wonderful. I'll bring the music. What's your favorite song?

VIOLET   Don't tell nobody, but I was always partial to "Down in the Valley." Guess it's because my first husband was always in and out of jail. Bootlegging.

EMMA   *(Laughing)*.  Yes, you are full of surprises.

VIOLET   Keeps me young.

*(LEE and GARNET enter, arm in arm.)*

Down in the valley
The valley so low
Hang your head over
Hear the wind blow

VIOLET  and EMMA
Hear the wind blow dear
Hear the wind blow
Hang your head over
Hear the wind blow

*(JOAN can be seen listening to this.)*

GARNET
Write me a letter
Containing three lines

ALL
Answer my question
Will you be mine...*(continues song a bit.)*.

GARNET   I seem to recall we made up our own lines to that.

LEE   Oh really?  *(LEE gets recorder from VIOLET.)*

*177*

GARNET   The roses love sunshine

VIOLET   You remember that?

GARNET   Honey, I'm cranky and lame but I'm not senile.

EMMA   I've got to hear this.  Sing it.

VIOLET   Garnet loves sunshine.

GARNET   Violet loves dew.

GARNET and VIOLET
Angels in heaven
know we'll be true
know we'll be true dear
know we'll be true
Angels in heaven
know we'll be true

VIOLET   That was when I was going to jail.

GARNET   Lawsy, Vi.  You didn't tell them about that did you?

LEE   About what?

VIOLET   Your Grandmother knows all about it.  We'll need to
get her permission for me to spill the beans.

LEE   Keeper of the family secrets?

VIOLET   Honey, I know a lot of secrets, a lot of information,
some of it useless.  But this is important - Take this down - If
you never remember anything else I've said or done, remember

this. I always assumed I had the right to any information, any truth, I wanted. If I didn't like what I found out, I learned not to take it personally. This freedom of speech goes two ways. I get to say what I want without getting put in jail. Although, I DID get put in jail. But I also get to HEAR what I want, READ what I want. Don't ever let anyone cut off your flow of information. You keep up with that women's history. This oral history. It's time we gave each other the information we need.

LEE   You are very special, Violet.

VIOLET   You put me in the shade, honey.

LEE   *(Hugging* VIOLET.*)*   Horsefeathers.

VIOLET   You have a good talk with your grandmother?

GARNET   We could solve the problems of the world, if they'd just listen to us.

*(*EMMA *looks to* LEE *who nods and smiles.)*

GARNET   *(Taking* LEE'S *arm.)*   You call me when you get there, hear? So I won't worry about you.   (GARNET *stuffs some money in* LEE'S *hand.)*   There. Some pin money.

LEE   Grandma, I can't take this.

GARNET   Help pay for all those waffles.   *(*LEE *gives* GARNET *a hug and kiss.)*

LEE   *(Holding* GARNET.)   I love you, Grandma.

GARNET   *(Patting her on the back.)*   I love you, too. And

don't you forget it. *(Turns to* EMMA *who gives her a hug.)*
You two take care of each other.

*(*LEE *hugs* VIOLET.*)*

EMMA   We will.

VIOLET   And don't be a stranger.

LEE   We'll be down for Christmas.

GARNET   We'll hold you to it.

LEE   Bye, Grandma. Take care.

GARNET   I will. You take care, too.

*(*EMMA *and* LEE *exit.)*

VIOLET   You can go with me, you know.

GARNET   I know.

VIOLET   I won't push you.

GARNET   You know how far that will get you.

VIOLET   True enough. What's wrong, Garnet? You seem off
somewhere.

GARNET   That Lee.

VIOLET   What about her?

GARNET   She told me about her and Emma.  I know you figured it out.

VIOLET   Does that bother you?

GARNET   Lawsy, no.

VIOLET   Then what is it?

GARNET   They have something I never had.  Did I live all this time for nothing?  I followed what everyone taught me.  I did what my parents told me to do.

VIOLET   You did not.

GARNET   MOST of the time I did what they taught me.

VIOLET   Don't regret the past, Garnet.  We had some wonderful times.  If we suffered, then it was worth it to give Lee and Emma more choices than we had.  If we compromissed, we still have each other and you have a granddaughter like Lee.

GARNET   I don't know what I'd do without you.

VIOLET   *(Putting her arm around* GARNET*)*   And I don't intend for you to find out.  I have to leave soon because I'm on the hotlines tonight.

GARNET   I don't know how you do it.  It would make me so mad.  I'd be out there stalking the alleys with my daddy's straight razor...*(slashing)*  performing operations.  No jury would convict me.

VIOLET   Garnet, you are a dangerous woman.

GARNET   Me?  Why I'm as weak as a kitten.

VIOLET   I've got just what the doctor ordered - your own kitchen and garden to putter in.

GARNET   Aren't you afraid I'll keel over in the daisies?

VIOLET   We'll hire some handsome muscular young men to do the heavy work.

GARNET   In that case, I'll want to get a new pair of glasses.

VIOLET   We'll have us some good times, Garnet.

GARNET   I know, honey.  We deserve it.

VIOLET   *(Kissing* GARNET*)*   You take care.

GARNET   You call as soon as you get home.

VIOLET   I will.  *(*GARNET *waves as* VIOLET *exits.)*


## SCENE FOURTEEN

*(The next morning.* EMMA *and* Lee *are having coffee on the porch.* EMMA *has been writing.)*

LEE   I'm glad I told her, Em.  I'm really glad.  She said it makes good practice, telling the truth.

EMMA   That's what you've always said.

LEE   But I thought it was an impossible ideal.

*182*

EMMA   Then let's go for the ideal.  No more compromises.

LEE   Gran said she was going to tell the truth as far back as she could take it.  What could she mean by that?

EMMA   She has her own secrets, Lee.

LEE   Gran?

EMMA   Nobody's perfect, love.  Wasn't it Lillian Hellman who said, "When you love, truly love, you take your chances on being hated by telling the truth"?

LEE   I couldn't hate her, no matter what her secret.

EMMA   No more than she could hate you for being my lover.

LEE   Got me, didn'tcha.

EMMA   It's good to see you smile.

LEE   Whatcha doin', huh?

EMMA   I thought of some new lines for Violet's party.

LEE   Sing them to me.

EMMA
This close to parting
From those we love
Shadows around us
Sweet as the dove
Sweet as the dove dear
Sweet as the dove

Shadows that whisper
There's always love

(EMMA *and* LEE *loosely freeze as* GARNET *can be heard singing.*)

GARNET
If you don't love me
Love whom you please
But throw your arms round me
Give my heart ease
Give my heart ease, dear
Give my heart ease
Throw your arms around me
Give my heart ease

(JOAN *is in the kitchen.*)

JOAN   *(Restless)*   Buffalo gals wontcha come out tonight...

(GARNET *appears in the doorway.*)

GARNET   Nice to hear music in the morning.

JOAN   I can't sing.

GARNET   If you can talk you can sing.  If you can walk you can dance. *(JOAN gives her a puzzled look)*   It's an African saying.

JOAN   *(Busying herself)*   I swear.  Open the door to Violet and you never know what kind of notions will come into your home.

GARNET   She is a catbird.  Kinda like Lee.

JOAN  No wonder...

GARNET  Yes?

JOAN  Oh, nothing.

GARNET  Could use some help.

*(JOAN pulls out a chair for GARNET and absent mindedly leaves her standing.)*

GARNET  What's riled you up?

JOAN  Me? Nothing.

GARNET  Nothing sure is responsible for a lot of bother around here.

JOAN  *(Seating GARNET)* I wish Lee had never started this oral history nonsense.

GARNET  I kinda like it. Talkin' about the old times. What's upset you?

JOAN  I don't imagine my worries interest you.

GARNET  You imagine wrong.

JOAN  Lee left me a tape of an interview with my father. He said he made two mistakes in his life. One was marrying my mother when he loved someone else. I never knew he didn't love her.

GARNET  We weren't so all-fired set on romance like you

younger ones were.  In my day, a woman got married because
that's what she was supposed to do.  There weren't choices.
Seems to me you're just like her in that respect.

JOAN We're not talking about me;we're talking about my father.

GARNET   That's right.

JOAN   Considering THAT mistake, what on earth could the
other one have been?  Do you know?

GARNET   Mebbe.

JOAN   Tell me.

GARNET   Don't know as I should.

JOAN   What harm could it do now?  I'll worry about it
constantly until you tell me.

GARNET   You always were good at worrying.  Your daddy
didn't care for Hays at all.  But you had your heart set on
marrying Hays and he didn't want to interfere.

JOAN   Why didn't he tell me?

GARNET   Didn't want you to spend your life caring for him.
Ending up a "lonely old maid".  I told him you would be the
daughter I'd never had and I'd be the mother you needed and that
rested his mind a little.  I didn't know you wouldn't trust me to
be a mother to you.

JOAN   Why should I?

GARNET   I still haven't died on you.

JOAN   You think I blame her for that?

GARNET   Yes.  All you know was that she left you.  Children don't understand death, else they'd never take a first step.

JOAN   How'd you get to be so wise?

GARNET   I'm a crone.  A woman gets old, all those years of listening bear fruit.

JOAN   Listening and caring and nursing and mending.

GARNET   Cooking and cleaning and crying when nobody's home.

JOAN   You cried alone?

GARNET   Some of it Hays' doing, some Eddy, some my own foolishness.

JOAN   We used to talk like this, didn't we.  When I was dating Hays.

GARNET I remember showing you how to fix his favorite meal.

JOAN   *(Laughs)*   Pot roast.  Must have given you all a jolt when you learned I was pregnant.

GARNET   Yes.  And Hays insisted on marrying you.

JOAN   Daddy said any man that set on marrying couldn't be all bad.

GARNET   I reckon Hays didn't want history repeating itself.

JOAN   What do you mean by that?

GARNET   Hays didn't tell you?

JOAN   Tell me what?

GARNET   I didn't marry until I was five.

GARNET   I was ignorant.  There's no other way to put it.
Violet had moved out of town and this handsome cousin of mine
paid me attention.  I didn't know any better.  When I found out I
was pregnant, I went to New York City, to stay with Violet, so
folks wouldn't know.  She helped me raise Hays until he was
five and I met Eddy on a visit back home.  Eddy didn't care like
some men would.  And when he got a job out of town, we
added five years to our wedding anniversary and let it be done.
But Hays knew.  Whenever we went to visit Hanging Rock he
heard about it.  Children can be so mean and it got so he didn't
want to go back there.

JOAN   What did your parents say?

GARNET   Nothin'.

JOAN   They weren't mad or...

GARNET   They were nothin'.  Didn't tell me how not to get
into a mess.  Didn't tell me how to get out of it.  I reckon they
prayed a lot.

JOAN   No wonder...It explains so much.  I'm glad you told me.

GARNET  Try not to throw it up to him.

JOAN  I wouldn't do that.

GARNET  'Preciate it; Violet has asked me to come live with her.

JOAN  I don't think Hays would like that.

GARNET  I'm not asking Hays. I'm asking you what you think.

JOAN  But Hays is your son.

GARNET  Sometimes a mother has to stop being a mother and be a woman.

JOAN  That sounds like something Lee would say.

GARNET  I may also dye my hair.

JOAN  Silver with electric blue stripes?

GARNET  Mebbe.

JOAN  (Rising)  Would you like a cup of coffee?

(LEE *and* EMMA *begin to sing softly: This close parting from those we love, shadows surround us sweet as a dove...).*

GARNET  That sounds real nice.

JOAN  Lee left some of that cinnamon flavored kind.

GARNET  Still have some pinwheels?

JOAN   I had saved some for Hays.  He left again for California this morning.

GARNET   Then he ain't here.

JOAN   *(Placing tin on table)*   He can have the box kind.

GARNET   We'll have ourselves a nice chat.

LEE and EMMA   Shadows that whisper,
                                    There's only love...

*(*JOAN *kisses* GARNET'S *cheek,* GARNET *pats her as lights fade.)*

◆◆◆◆◆◆◆◆◆◆◆◆◆◆◆◆◆◆◆◆◆◆◆◆◆◆◆◆◆◆◆◆◆◆◆

Three of PAMELA SIMONES' plays have been presented at Cleveland Public Theatre's New Play Festival.  Her play about the Bronte sisters, FROST FROM FIRE, has been performed by the University of Miami.  Showcased by the Actors and Playwright's Theater in Akron, her works deal with women, and issues such as the realities of aging (EVERYWOMAN, a contemporary satire complete with music and slapstick comedy; Mother Nature is a character in this drama), and the significance oral tradition (SINS OF THE MOTHERS).  A Vassar graduate, Pam is a librarian at Kent Free Library, and lives in Akron, Ohio with her three cats.  She is the Low Budget Theatre Company's playwright in residence.

*Flood II*

*Photo by Ellen Symons*

# Needlepoint and Cross Stitch

*Phyllis RoseChild creates figures in needlepoint and cross stitch patterns. She and her lifepartner of five years, Sharon, work together on many of her projects co-creating concepts, design and color coordination. Both women say it takes patience and concentration, but it's fun and rewarding. Phyllis works as a supervisor in a non-traditional occupation through which she utilizes her varied skills. Since the purchase of their new home in the suburbs, she has installed a gas line for a gas range and completed electric wiring for an overhead fan.*

*Oftimes her subjects are symbolic such as the "BETTY" depicted below. An original design, Phyllis decided on Betty because, she says, "That was a lesbian code name in former times." The double female symbols are mauve and pink.*

192

*Tiny female symbols offer meaning/background embellishment.
"As a child my grandmother used to encourage handicrafts; in
those days women had to embroider color onto their linens and
pillowcases to put color into them. And it's easy ~ trace the
form onto a matting or you can draw your own. Select colors
and then relax and begin stitching. At completion, you block
and trim the edges." Phyllis has a penchant for Flamingos.
Whether in the form of mobile, wallpaper, or needlepoint,
flamingos decorate their bathroom, bedroom, parlor and den.*

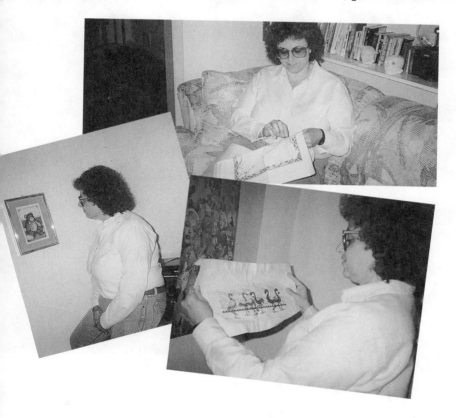

# POTTERY

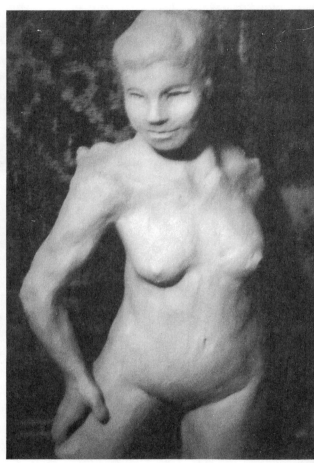

# AND
# SCULPTURE

*POTTERY AND SCULPTURE BY CINDY HARDIN*

*For centuries, before the beginning of recorded time, women
have created lovely, and of course, practical, arts and crafts.
Cindy and her lifepartner(l), Zel Bowers, sell their pottery at
Lesbian Fairs (recent one East Coast Lesbian Festival, 1993).*

*Cindy talks about her background and values:  "I was raised
in San Diego, California.  At 20, I joined the Army and was
sent to the only place I didn't ask for - Texas.  I stayed in
Austin for two years, then headed back to San Diego again.
Following a lover, I ended up in Columbus, Georgia in 1980.
I work teaching crafts and setting up classes and workshops
for Britt David Studios.  My major media is sculpture in clay.
I do other things such as painting, weaving, photography,
paper making, silk screening, printing and I'm currently
working on stained glass and baskets.  I gravitate to the earthy
colors and textures, trying to let the media show me what it
wants to be rather than forcing it into something.  I was asked
once why I went into art.  Because I didn't have an answer
and just for fun, I said, "Power".  Years later, I realized what
I meant:  SELF-EMPOWERMENT.  How wonderful to be
able to take a brush and paint or a lump of clay and be able to
make people see and more important feel something.  Unlike
everchanging words, visual art holds a timeless power of its
own.  I have spent my whole life watching faces and making
faces out of everything around.  Animal faces, dwarf faces,
strange distorted ones, soft and gentle ones.  I still play with*

195

the grain of wood, the shapes of leaves, the powder on the bathroom floor. I used to feel my art had no purpose except as something nice to look at until recently. After I was attacked in my home a few years ago, I experienced flashbacks, not only of the attack, but of childhood abuse I suffered as well. I found that unknowingly I have always been looking for the strange look of the survivor in all of the faces I have seen. I I try to give my faces the power and strength of someone who has not just existed, but also has lived after the hurt and loss of an abuse. Little by little, as I discover the stories and the life and strength in the clay, in the plaster and paint in my art, I see what I have been looking for. If just once in a while I can share my feeling of safety, joy, loss and sadness, and above all, the strength inside us all, I've done OK. Beauty can and does come despite the pain.

*- Cindy Hardin*

# APRIL ANN TORRES

*Oil Painting/Photo by April Ann Torres*

Artist APRIL ANN TORRES has two photos in this anthology:
"OUT to Play" (opp. WHERE THE SENORITAS ARE) and "Natural
on Natural" (above), both paintings oil on rag cotton. A 32 year-
old resident in Long Beach, California, April entered Art Center
College of Design at 27 as an illustration major and graduated in
1990. She currently works as in-house art studio manager/
illustrator, which of course allows her to support her painting
habit. She explains, "Portrait painting allows me to explore the
personality of an individual. I am fascinated by the silent
unconscious moment of another's existence - Why do we have
the ability to create, see, ponder, imagine? What is the original
purpose of art? For me it is about what I get out of the act of
painting, taking the time from our incredibly fast-paced society, to
create. Recently I have embarked on a body of work that is about
exploring my personal visual language, the language of the
subconscious mind. This kind of work exercises that raw impulse
to create from the soul, bringing me closer to myself. It is a bonus
to leave evidence of this experience.

*197*

Photo by Ana R. Kissed
Self-Portrait Looking at Self Portrait, '84

# MANCHILD
## by Ira L. Jeffries

## CHARACTERS

HARRY HALL   *A Retired Trucker*

NICOLE HALL (NIKKI)   *An Airplane Pilot*


## ACT ONE

## SCENE ONE

*The time is the 1990's in the living room of Harry Hall, a businessman trucker. He is watching a football game and drinking beer; the doorbell rings at the wrong time of the game. He curses a little as he rises, and backs out of the room so not to miss anything.*

HARRY   Who is it?

NIKKI   It's me daddy, Nikki.

(HARRY *opens the door to his daughter* NIKKI, *an airplane pilot in her captain's uniform.*)

HARRY   Ooh, it's my daughter the big time airlines pilot. Well come in, come in my game is on and it's the last quarter.

NIKKI   Hi, daddy, surprised to see me?

HARRY   Sure, sure I am but my game is on Nikki.  Come on

in and close the door.

(*A quick slip and missed kiss between them, and* HARRY *hurries back to the television set and resumes his seat as* NIKKI *stands watching him and shaking her head.*)

NIKKI   Are you sure it's alright if I stay or should I make an appointment?

HARRY   (*Waving at her*)  Wait!  Wait!  It's almost over.

NIKKI   I presume that means that you want me to stay.

HARRY   Of course, of course and that's if you have the time captain sir.

(NIKKI *looks at her father and rolls her eyes upwards and sighs.  She sets her flight bag down, takes off her jacket, hangs it on the back of a chair and makes herself comfortable.  She entertains herself by walking around the room looking at familiar items.  She notices something new.*)

NIKKI   I don't remember seeing this before daddy, is this...

HARRY   Nikki please!

(HARRY *waves frantically for her to be quiet and* NIKKI *responds by mimicking him and rolling her eyes at her father. Finally, the game is over and* HARRY *cuts off the television set. Meanwhile,* NIKKI *has left the room for the kitchen.*)

HARRY   Well, that was a good game, I mean those Bears kick butt all over the place.  Do you know that's the first time I have ever...

(HARRY *turns and notices* NIKKI's *absence.*)

Nikki! Nikki! Where are you?

NIKKI (OS) I'm in the kitchen boiling water for some tea, want some?

HARRY Want some what, some tea? Please, just bring me a beer captian Nikki.

NIKKI (OS) Daddy, you know that you shouldn't be drinking any alcohol with your pressure and all.

HARRY Just bring me a beer Nikki and don't be telling me about shoulds and shouldn'ts, I'm the parent here.

(NIKKI *enters with a small tray with tea pot, cup and saucer and sugar cubes and* HARRY's *beer. She sets the tray down hands him his beer, sits and pours her tea.* HARRY *watches her intently as he sips his beer.*)

HARRY When are you going to settle down and marry a real man instead of a career? I want some grands.

NIKKI Then maybe you should have some.

HARRY Oh cut, cute. A woman shouldn't be so successful, not like a man. A woman's real place is in the home, to marry, pro-create, and make a man a good wife. So there, I've had my say.

NIKKI Oh, is that so. The way you brought me up with all that rough and tumble stuff as if I were a manchild instead of a girl. And now you expect me to become a drudge like mama? Daddy please now.

HARRY   A drudge?  A drudge you say?  Your mother loved being my wife.  God bless her soul.  (HARRY *and* NIKKI *make the sign of the cross*)  I was a good husband and father.  Who provided the music lessons, good clothes and shoes, trips, and that fancy college education which made you want to do men's work?

NIKKI   Don't get me started daddy.  Are you inferring that I've taken on the role of a man because I've become an airline pilot?  Oh, daddy, you're such an obstinate and narrow minded macho fool.  You provided me with the things a father should provide for his child.  Plenty of encouragement yes, but closeness and understanding, mama gave me that because she wanted me to make sure I had more options than she had.  She didn't want me dependent on a man for everything like she was, and become an unfulfilled woman.

HARRY   Who are you calling a fool, Nikki?  And your mother was not unfulfilled, God bless her soul.  (*Once more, they cross themselves.*)

NIKKI   And I resent your inference that I have taken on a man's role just because I'm a pilot.  It's an affront to me as a woman.  It's unfortunate that I was born a girl because I know you wanted a manchild.

HARRY   (*Defensively*)  I never said that!

NIKKI   No, not in so many words but why else would you buy me train sets, marbles, pants instead of dresses until mama took charge, and the rough housing with me as you would a son, and get mad when I cried and called me a sissy.  And the car, remember the little red car you bought me when I was five?

*202*

HARRY  (*Reminiscing*)  Oh yes, the car, that little red car. Oh, you looked so cute peddling up and down the block in your khaki snowsuit.

NIKKI  Yes, cute indeed, and those damn boxing lessons.

HARRY  (*Becoming defensive again*)  I wanted you to learn how to defend yourself, after all, you were a girl.

NIKKI  Only a girl.  See what I mean daddy, only a girl.  And what the hell is that supposed to mean, huh daddy, huh?

HARRY  (*Attempting to vindicate himself*)  What I mean is...

NIKKI  You mean that you think women are weak and not as good as men except for cooking, cleaning, having babies, and you know what else.

HARRY  (*Becoming somewhat intimidated by* NIKKI's *accusations*)  Now you stop talking like that to your father in that tone of voice or I'll...

NIKKI  (*Narrowing her eyes and placing her hands on her hips*) ...or you'll what daddy.  Punch my lights out or something?

(HARRY *jumps up from his chair confronting his daughter.*)

HARRY  I could you know, maybe it would teach you a real lesson about your fresh mouth!

NIKKI  Hmph, I think you had just better sit back down and drink your beer daddy.

(NIKKI *turns away, picks up her tea to drink and her father*

203

*playfully attacks her from behind causing her to spill some of her tea.)*

HARRY   Come on, come on, you think that you're so tough Ms. Airline pilot, come on.

NIKKI   Daddy, are you insane?  I'm a grown woman now, I don't play like that anymore!

(HARRY *keeps egging her on and begins bouncing her around like a boxer, cuffing her here and there.  She merely ducks his harmless blows in the beginning and then she takes him on taking a boxer's stance, beginning to bob and weave in earnest.)*

So you want to play rough huh?  Well alright, you've got it.

(NIKKI *bobs and weaves circling her fatgher looking for an opening.  Finally, she hooks him with a left to the stomach doubling him over and a right to the jab.  Stunned, he falls to the floor.)*

HARRY   Nikki, you  hit your father.

NIKKI   Well, you started it daddy, you started it.  I'm a woman, a damn good woman who happened to chose a well paying profession in a man's world, and I had to fight like hell to qualify.  You taught me to go after what I wanted in life and not to take second best to anyone, man or woman.  If becoming a pilot, and kicking your butt qualifies me as a manchild in your sight then you're mistaken daddy and totally out of touch with reality and the times.  (NIKKI *picks up teapot and enters the kitchen for more hot water.  HARRY, still in shock about his daughter decking him lay on the floor rubbing his jaw.  Finally he rises, holding his stomach.)*

HARRY   Phew!  Nikki really knocked the poop out of me. (*Picks up his beer and drinks the rest of the contents, then sits, deeply in thought.*)   Nikki's right.  I guess I have been a little insensitive and acting like a real shit head.  Wow!  She's really got some punch.  (*Strokes his jaw gingerly and begins to smile.*) Nicole?  Nicole honey.

NIKKI   (*Enters the living room.*)  Who are you calling? (*looks in the direction of the other room.*)  Is someone else here besides us?

HARRY   Of course not, I'm calling you.  Isn't that your name, honey?

NIKKI   Honey?  Of course it's my name but you haven't called me Nicole since...in fact, you have never called me Nicole.

HARRY   Yeah, yeah, I know, I know.  I wanted to name you Nick after your grandmother but your mother wouldn't hear of it, so we compromised and she chose Nicole.  But Nicole sounded nice too..too...

NIKKI   Too feminine for macho man Harry Hall, right daddy?

HARRY   Now, now Nicole, let's not argue about it.  Maybe I have been a little unreasonable.

NIKKI   Unreasonable is not the word.  How's your jaw, did I hurt you? (*Approaches her father, sits on the arm of his chair and puts her arm around his shoulders.*)

HARRY   Oh, it's alright I guess but you do pack a wallop captain lady.  (NIKKI *hugs and kisses her father on sore jaw.*)

NIKKI   You know daddy, I always wanted to please you because you set such high standards for me, so I went for a profession I thought would make you proud of me but instead, the sarcasm and the arguments began to escalate between us.

HARRY   Maybe it was because I became a little jealous and envious of your success Nicole.  I've always had high aspirations myself but being a black man in America blocked me at practically every turn.  That's why I started my own trucking business so that I could support my family, maintain my self esteem and create my own success and not have to depend on a living ass for anything.

NIKKI   Oh daddy, I never knew.  You never told me.

HARRY   A man doesn't talk to his daughter about things like that.

NIKKI   And why not, I'm talkable.

HARRY   I'm sure you are honey, but that's how we men are. We act out our feelings and frustrations, and transfer our dream onto our children without their really understanding the plan. I'm sorry for all the unkind words and innuendo's.  Yes, I did want a son and though I may have raised you with a son in mind, I loved you, and I am proud of you.

(*A tender moment between them.*)

Now, what about those grands Nikki?

NIKKI   (*Gets up and pours her tea.*)  I don't think there will be any daddy.

HARRY   Are you sterile or something?

NIKKI   Daddy, women aren't sterile, only men are and no, there's nothing wrong physically but I am...something...

HARRY   Alright, so you're not sterile or whatever women are but you're something.  Now, what's that supposed to mean?

NIKKI   It means that I'm a lesbian.

HARRY   A what?  What's that, a new religion like buddhism or something like that?

NIKKI   No, no, no it's none of that...oh daddy, you're making this very difficult for me.  *(Rattles on quickly)*  I wanted to be like you, strong, forceful, independent, in charge of my life.  I loved mama but I didn't want to be a housewife, and she didn't want me to be either.

HARRY   Alright, what's the big deal, so you won't marry. These are different times and you're of another generation.  You dont' have to get married if you don't want to, but what's this lesbian thing got to do with your giving me some grands?

NIKKI   This lesbian thing as you put it means that you'll never have grands because I'll never have a man in my life in a sexual way.

HARRY   What do you mean you'll never have a man in your life, you're surrounded by men all the time!

NIKKI   Daddy, listen to me.  I like women okay, that's what a lesbian is.

*207*

HARRY   You mean...(*looks at her real hard as it finally sinks in*) you mean that...nah, you don't mean that, I know you don't mean that...

NIKKI   Oh yes I do, I mean just that.

HARRY   (*Rises, walks around and attempts to say something but words do not come.  He scratches his head, looks at her, turns away, mumbles to himself in disbelief about his daughter being a lesbian.*)   Look Nikki, I don't care what you call yourself or how I may have raised you, you're still not a man, and I can out fuck you any day.

NIKKI   How dare you speak like that to me!  Well, I got it daddy, and I see you got it too.

HARRY   Why didn't you keep it to yourself?  Why did you have to tell me?

NIKKI   Because I got sick and tired of you bugging me about marriage and giving you grands.  Furthermore I wanted you to know, I didn't want to live a life of deception, and after all, I am your daughter.

HARRY   You're no daughter of mine.  Your mother gave birth to you, I merely planted the seed...maybe.

NIKKI   Yeah, you're right daddy.  I understand, I don't like what you've said but I do understand the hurt, confusion and disappointment you're experiencing.  Maybe if you hadn't pressed me, I may have delayed telling you a little longer but I did intend to tell you one day anyhow.  (*Takes final sip of tea and places everything on the tray.*)   May I bring you another beer?

HARRY   *(Looks at her hard before answering.)*  Bring me two.

NIKKI   *(Enters the kitchen with her tray and emerges with two beers.  She hands him one and sets the other beside him.  He drinks the first one down, picks up the other and drinks that one down as well.  She puts on her jacket, picks up her flight bag.)*

NIKKI   I'm flying out tonight.  I'll see you when I return next week, that is if you want to see me. *(He doesn't answer.  She approaches him, hugs and kisses him and starts to exit.)* Goodbye, daddy.   See you next week?

HARRY   I'll be here   (NIKKI *exits and* HARRY *just sits there in deep thought.  Slowly, he begins to smile.)*  Oh, well, I guess I have a son after all.

*Sculpture/Photo by Cindy Hardin*

**Photo by Lisa M. Wright**

*Clotel smiles reminiscing some fond memories as she focuses
momentarily into the direction of her ex-lover*
*- CLOTEL, A Love Story*

# CLOTEL, A LOVE STORY

## *by Ira L. Jeffries*

**CHARACTERS**

CLOTEL   *A woman aged 40 - 45 years old (black or white)*

*The time is 1960. A bare stage setting, with a street backdrop of a row of brownstones and a physical stoop. Sitting on the stoop is CLOTEL, a very attractive woman 30 - 35 years old, dressed in a dress of the mid 50's, high heels, stockings, and her hair done up in a style popular for the 60's. She sits on the stoop idling the time away waving at and speaking to passers by and her neighbors. Her mood is sort of bored melancholia. As she sits with her chin resting in the cup of her hand looking around at nothing in particular, her attention focuses on a woman walking towards her. Her bright intense eyes widen in disbelief as she follows the woman up the block. The woman glances in CLOTEL's direction as she passes and for a few brief seconds their eyes meet. CLOTEL, not wishing to be recognized, drops her head. The woman appears to recognize her, calls her name.*

WOMAN'S VOICE OVER   Clotel?  Is that you Clotel?

*(CLOTEL doesn't respond and keeps her eyes riveted to the ground. The woman walks a little closer for a better look, scrutinizing CLOTEL intently and then apologizes.)*

WOMAN'S VOICE OVER   Please forgive the impoliteness of staring miss but you looked so familiar I thought that I knew you.

*(The* WOMAN *walks away as* CLOTEL, *with head still bowed follows her out of the corner of her eye until she is out of sight.)*

CLOTEL   She recognized me, or should I say she thought she recognized me.  It must have been my eyes...she used to love my eyes...used to say that mine were the most beautiful eyes she had ever seen.

(CLOTEL *smiles reminiscing some fond memories as she focuses momentaily into the direction of her ex-lover.)*

She used to be my lover you know and we were very much in love, and I loved her so much...maybe too much and that's why I lost her...I guess it's hard to believe a sad, forlorn almost middle aged woman dressed in this old dress could have been a lover of such caliber and class...but I did and she loved me too.

(CLOTEL *runs her fingers lightly over her clothing.*)  This used to be a real nice dress once, one of my favorites.  *(Once more she runs her hands over her clothing as if she were wearing fine silk.)*

I find it hard to believe myself; what have I come to...welfare and a two by four room with a sink thank God...I still have some pride and I like to be clean...but I used to be georgeous and I had clothes galore.

(CLOTEL's *mood turns from melancholia to sassy.  Light change here as she comes out of her worn and shabby shawl that cover her vintage dress; this reveals a very shapely figure with great legs.  She begins to simulate talking to the club inhabitants, avoiding their grasping hands, flirting with others.)*

I mean I was so fine that the butches used to fight over me all

*212*

the time...oh, it was bedlam in that club where I used to hand...it was wild, absolutely wild!...and I thrived on all that attention...when I walked in, all the single butches used to crowd around me...even the butches in domestic situations used do follow my every move with lustful eyes...very discreetly, of course, so their old ladies wouldn't notice...but they noticed and they used to hate my guts!   (CLOTEL *laughs heartily.*)  I could tell what all the butches in the club were thinking...all but her.

*(Lights change to a spot and she focuses her attention in the direction that her ex-lover used to sit.)*

She would stop by the club frequently for drinks...always sitting in the same spot...feeding the juke box and watching everyone perform...that's right, perform!...because that's what we were, performers...trying to out do each other...out dress, out laught, out drink and out love each other...oh, it was a wild scene, really wild...oh there were a lot of other fine and very beautiful sisters in the club but I was the finest and the most beautiful.

*(Movement and action by her throughout this scene as she describes her interaction with the club inhabitants.)*

When I would come prancing into that club in my high heels like Aunt Hester's pet pony, all of those butches would be vying for my attention...calling my name, ordering me drinks, crowding around me, touching my a..(CLOTEL *clears her throat at the faux pas she almost made.)*    ...uh, my personal anatomy, you know what I mean...I said, uh, uh, uh, no free feels around here baby...you can have it all if the price is right...now don't get me wrong, that's just a metaphor...it's just that my time was too valuable to be taken as a cheap whore for some drinks, some reefer and some blow, uh, uh, you see, my philosophy is that a woman is precious and should be treated as such I always say...you had to keep your priorities straight with those women because they were tough, hard street butches who would jack you up to get their way...but they didn't mess with me because they knew I carried a .22 and would put a bullet in their ass if necessary...oh yes, you really had to keep your priorities straight with those women...some of them were so cheap, they would try and get in your panties for a bottle of beer...but her, she was different somehow, very different...she was like no other butch I had ever met in my life...she was intriguing...I just had to get to know her, and I did too...now, that was the biggest mistake I ever made because I fell in love...for the first time in my life, I fell in love...she just blew my mind with her smooth, a suave sophistication...she wasn't one of us...she was...how would you say...an enigma, and not all like the other's...I could deal with them...never got caught up in no love thing...it wasn't my style...but her, she spoke a language my ears had never heard...and her clothes...veeeery sophisticated, elegant suits, custom made shirts, little silk ties and black suede shoes...oh! those shoes she wore...she was always pressed, looking like brand new money...umph!...she was sharp, real sharp...the butches at the club became jealous when I started paying her so much attention...they used to refer to her as that corporate Negro, just because the woman was college educated and had her own Harlem law office...they would say to me..."Clotel, you're stepping out of your league, girl...that butch is from an entirely different world from ours...she ain't really colored, negro or black for that matter, she's only slumming until she moves further up in the corporate world, and Harlem and you become history." - corporate Negro!...jealous, just jealous and envious that's all...some black people make me sick, always coming down on their people with their narrow-minded prejudices!...To hell with those Negroes, I took up with her anyway and we became real close and that's when I started to change...I wanted her to be proud of me...I began to dress more conservatively, and on occasion, she would take me into her world...you know, parties, luncheon's at art galleries, concerts and even the opera...can you imagine, me, Clotel at the Metropolitan Opera House?...I changed drastically trying to fit in...so much so I began to talk like them, think like them and act like them...I became a class act...now I've always had class but I became classier with more finesse and style...oh, I was so proud of myself that I had successfully made the transition into her world...I felt like another person, the femme that I used to be no longer existed...my world was a total turn around...I still used to stop by the club on occasion and have a few with my former associates but even though my lover still frequented the club, she became increasingly puzzled as to why I no longer cared to...she began to notice the change in my demeanor, and how well I fit into her world and she began to act differently towards me...becoming more distant and aloof...but when we made love it was still wonderful and exciting and I kew that she still loved me, she was gentle, passionate and oh so tender...it was as if she were making love to a fragile flower...handling me just so...oh, how I loved her, but after the lovemaking, she became distant...I would snuggle up to her soft, warm moist body and she would hold me in her arms, just so.

*(This scene should be very demonstrative.)*

...But she wasn't there for me any longer...finally, I got up the nerve to question her about this aloofness towards me and she admitted that she didn't like the change in me...the new me...she said..."I was attracted to you because you were different from the other women I've known...you had depth, color, vibrancy, character, and now you've become like them...shallow, plastic, superficial and mediocre." ...mediocre, she called me shallow and mediocre." *(Hurt and angry.)* After she finished reading me, she turned away, but I was persistent, I wasn't going to let her off the hook that easily so I said, "But you make love to me as though you still loved me." Oh, I still love you she said, "but not the you that you have become, understand?" I was devastated by this cruel revelation, after all, I merely wanted her to be proud of me to fit into her world...plastic, shallow, superficial...I guess I tried too hard...as she became more and more distant, we drifted apart because I didn't want to change...I had become accustomed to my new friends and environment and for awhile, I continued to circulate in my new world...but it wasn't the same anymore without her...I (CLOTEL *places her shabby worn shawl around her and sinks back into her melancholia and returns to sit on the stoop.*) I lost my job, my apartment and most of my beautiful clothes except for a few things...and this. (CLOTEL *runs her hand over her elegant worn dress.*) I didn't return to my former world, I couldn't because I didn't belong there anymore...I guess you could say that I became a drifter, moving from rooming house to rooming house...not even begging for a living just sitting in one place looking pitiful and sorry...I didn't want anything anymore but her...only her.

(CLOTEL *looks in the direction her ex-lover went and notices her coming back down the street.*)

Oh, my God, here she comes again (CLOTEL *immediately drops her head again, staring at the ground. Her ex-lover stops in front of her.*)

WOMAN'S VOICE OVER This one is for you. (WOMAN *places something in* CLOTEL's *lap and moves on.* CLOTEL *maintains her position until she's sure she had gone. She examines the item and see's only a wad of bills with a rubber band around it. She explodes in anger.*)

CLOTEL  Money?  She gives me money?  I don't want her goddamn money or her pity!  *(Starts throwing the money away when she feels something hard and resistant.)*  What's this?  Another token of her pity? (CLOTEL *unwraps the money from around the object.  It is a small cardboard framed picture of clotel and her ex-lover, one they had taken when they first met ten years ago.  CLOTEL's entire mood changes.  She begins to smile and cry and becomes very emotional as she stares at the photograph.)*  She really did recognize me, it's a picture of us that we took in the Penny Arcade on 125th Street when we first met...ten years ago.  *(Perks up now considerably, wiping her eyes and anxiously looks in the direction her ex-lover had gone.)*

CLOTEL  She cares, she still cares.  Maybe she'll come back.  Oh, I'm such a mess. (CLOTEL *carefully lays the picture down, sticks the money in her bosom, removes the shabby, worn shawl from around her shoulders, flings it on the stoop and begins to wipe her face, straighten her clothing, smoothes her hair into place, and props her lovely legs on the stoop to straighten her stockings.  While she is preoccupied, her ex-lover returns and watches her momentarily.)*

WOMAN'S VOICE OVER  You look just fine Cotel, you're still a beauty and I've missed you.  Oh, how I've missed you.

CLOTEL  *(Keeps her back turned to her ex-lover.)*  But I've aged!

WOMAN'S VOICE OVER  Yes, but like the finest wine of which you know I'm a connoisseur.

CLOTEL  Have you really missed me?

WOMAN'S VOICE OVER  Terribly, more than you could ever

imagine. I've been out of the country for years on business, and I couldn't get back, if I had, I would have found you long ago. Forgive me for being an insensitive fool?

CLOTEL   *(turns to face her ex-lover.)*   Of course, my darling, of course.

*(The lovers embrace warmly and start to walk off.   CLOTEL stops suddenly as if remembering something.)*

CLOTEL   My picture!

(CLOTEL *returns to the stoop, picks up the little photograph and rejoins her lover as they stroll offstage.   As they exit, the lights focus on the shawl and then a slow fade out.*)

◆◆◆◆◆◆◆◆◆◆◆◆◆◆◆◆◆◆◆◆◆◆◆◆◆◆◆◆◆◆◆◆◆◆◆◆◆◆◆◆◆

**IRA L. JEFFRIES, 61, African-American playwright, artistic director, producer, professional journalist and founder of KALEIDOSCOPE THEATRE COMPANY is a graduate of the City College of New York with a B.A. in Communications. As a journalist, she has written extensively for the lesbian and gay print media which includes: QW Magazine (formerly NYQ); SAPPHOS ISLE; WOMANEWS and B&G Magazine. Ira's works have also appeared in Joan Nestle's anthology, THE PERSIS-TENT DESIRE - A FEMME/BUTCH READER. She has been writing plays for fifteen years and has written over ten plays dealing with lesbian/gay and universal issues. Her Motto - One step at a time, and faith ... leads me to my ultimate goal - SUCCESS.   IRA L. JEFFRIES** *Photo by Morgan Grenwald*

*218*

# Portrait of Lisa M. Wright

*Photographer, LISA M. WRIGHT recently graduated from Macalester College in St. Paul with a degree in Cultural Anthropology. She says, "I am currently doing a number of odd jobs and working on my photography business. Besides photography, my greatest passions are horses and playing rugby." Her collection of beautiful greeting cards can be mail ordered. Just write: Imagine Images, PO Box 6l20, Minn, Mn. 55406.*

## About the photos:

*~WOMAN IN WINDOW OF TENEMENT (opp. CLOTEL) - "I was over at a friend's house one summer's eve and went outside to figure out where to do some portraits of her. I got the idea for this photo when she looked out of the window, waving, silhouetted by the inside light. To me, this symbolized being caught in the world that we live in but longing for something else, a better world, and looking for escape. The world inside is brightly lit, safe, while outside is a dark, difficult path to follow. The figure in the window gazes into that darkness, searching, and reaching beyond the mainstream "ism" ladden society."*

*~SELF PORTRAIT (back cover photo) - "I used a tripod and cable-release shutter to take this photo of me facing away from the camera kissing. I also used a filter to soften the image."*

*~MEREDITH PLAYING POOL -"This photo is of my best friend and roommate Meredith (aka Dude) engaged in one of her favorite pastimes. I love to watch her play, with all her attitude, quick witty humor, and beauty. We have spent many o'wild nights together in a hazy, queer, local bar..."*

*WOMAN BY SHED - "I took this photo at my lover Nancy's home in Michigan. Although she lives right off a main road, the house is alongside a small river, nestled into woodlands, giving the illusion of being in the country. I liked the way the shed looked, its air of nostalgia, and the play of light and shadows on it. Nancy fit the rustic setting well, dressed in her baggy overalls, white tee and hat so I took some shots of her..."*

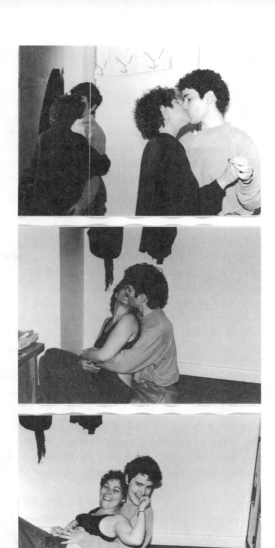

*Photo by Ellen Symons*

*"Okay. I've always been very clear about our
relationship...But now that you're doing this dating
thing...well...my heart has been doing different things...I mean,
ah...not only my heart, but my whole body.*
*- THE SECRET LIFE OF PLANTS*

# THE SECRET LIFE OF PLANTS *by Pam Cady*

## CHARACTERS

ROBIN

ALTHEA

LESLIE

## SCENE ONE

*Lights dark. From offstage comes the sound of a car as it pulls up outside. Two doors slam. Keys jingle in the lock and ROBIN enters. She reaches to her left and turns on the light. She is beautifully dressed and is obviously coming home after an evening out. ALTHEA enters the room after her and shuts the door. ROBIN ignores her and takes off her high heeled shoes on her way to the bedroom SL.)*

ALTHEA   So you're just going to ignore me?

ROBIN   I'm not ignoring you.  *(She exits into the bedroom.)*

ALTHEA   You're not ignoring me?

ROBIN   *(Offstage)*   If I was ignoring you, I wouldn't be talking to you, would I?

ALTHEA   Oh, I see.  This is your passive agressive stage on the way to ignoring me.  Right?  Robin? *(She waits for an answer. There is none forthcoming)* Now, you're ignoring me. *(Still no answer)* Great! *(Beat)* What could I do? *(No answer)* Fine. *(Silence)* This is really ridiculous, Robin. I don't even know why you're angry. Will you just come out and talk to me? *(Still nothing)* Okay, be that way. Obviously you'll just tell me when you're ready. *(ALTHEA sits on the couch and waits for a few moments.)* You know, two can play this game. I can ignore you too. *(She picks up a magazine from the coffee table in front of her. She flips through it, occasionally glancing off to the bedroom to check on ROBIN. She's obviously tense however, and the magazine can not hold her attention. She puts the magazine back on the table and stands up.)* God. I hate this shit! *(To the bedroom)* It drives me crazy. You know this makes me crazy. I can't believe that an otherwise very healthy and adult woman as to withhold her feelings like a child holding her breath when she doesn't get her own way. *(She has been pacing, but now stops and faces bedroom.)* That's exactly what you're doing you know - you're holding your emotional breath so you'll get your own way. and it's working, okay? You can stop now - I give up, you're right. I'm wrong, I'm sorry; you can come out now. *(She waits several moments, but gets no answer. She walks over to the door, wrenches it open and then slams it, staying inside the apartment. She leans against the door with her arms folded and waits. A few moments later, ROBIN enters with a towel wrapped around her head and Noxema spread over her entire face. She has changed into a long white terry cloth robe. She is adjusting the towel over her head so she does not realize that ALTHEA is still in the apartment. She crosses to the kitchenette SR.. ALTHEA crosses center stage, watching her. ROBIN opens the refrigerator door with her back to ALTHEA. She leans in to grab a soda.)* If I hadn't slammed the door, you would have hibernated all night?

ROBIN   Gees, Althea.  Give me a fucking heart attack why don't you?  I thought you left.

ALTHEA   I know you did.  (*Beat*)   What is going on with you?  Why are you so mad at me?

ROBIN   I'm not mad at you.

ALTHEA   (*Snorts*)  You're not mad at me?

ROBIN   It's true.  I'm not MAD at you.

ALTHEA   Alright, if you're not MAD at me, then what are you?

ROBIN   Look, I'm not prepared to talk about it right now.  I'm not even sure what's going on.  Okay?

ALTHEA   God.  I hate it when you do this.

ROBIN   What?  Do what?

ALTHEA   You're obviously upset with me in some way - I mean you stop talking to me - and then when you do start talking to me again you won't talk to me.

ROBIN   I told you if you would listen.  I just need time to think things over for myself, okay?

ALTHEA   (*Pause*)   Can I guess?

ROBIN   No; will you stop?  Gees, Althea, you're like some dog with a bone.  Drop it, will you?  Why don't you go home and get some sleep.  I'll call you tomorrow morning.

ALTHEA   Yeah, well, I'm going out tomorrow morning.

ROBIN   I thought we were having brunch tomorrow morning.

ALTHEA   I know.  But if you'd been talking to me I would have asked you if you minded if I cancelled.

ROBIN   But we have brunch every Saturday morning.  We never cancel.

ALTHEA   That isn't true.  A few months ago you couldn't make it.

ROBIN   That's because Leslie and I were breaking up and I had to help her move out.   You were there, you helped her move out too.

ALTHEA   Well, you couldn't make it, could you?

ROBIN   No, you're right, Althea, I couldn't make it.

ALTHEA   So I'm not going to be able to make it tomorrow, okay?

ROBIN   Why not?  What are you doing?

ALTHEA   (*Does not want to discuss this.  Mumbles*)   I'm going for a bike ride.

ROBIN   What?  I didn't hear you.

ALTHEA   I'm just going for a bike ride.  I'll call you when I get home, okay?

ROBIN   A bike ride?  You don't even own a bicycle.

ALTHEA   I know that, Robin.  I'm borrowing one.

ROBIN   Why are you going on a bike ride?

ALTHEA   Because I want to.  *(Beat)*  Because somebody imvited me to go, alright?

ROBIN   Is this a date?

ALTHEA   Is it okay if we don't discuss this right now?

ROBIN   You're standing me up for an exercise date?  You hate to exercise.  You won't even take a walk on the beach.

ALTHEA   I'm not standing you up.  We have brunch every Saturday morning.  I didn't think you'd mind if I skipped it this one time.  But if it bothers you that much, I'll call and cancel.

ROBIN   Okay.  I'll see you tomorrow morning.

ALTHEA   Okay?  Robin.

ROBIN   What?

ALTHEA   I can't believe you're making me cancel.

ROBIN   I'm not making you cancel.  You suggested it.

ALTHEA   Yeah, but not because I want to, because it bothers you.

ROBIN   Well, for God's sakes, don't cancel for me, only do it if you want to.

ALTHEA   Gees, Althea, I will not be mad at you.  I'll be a little disappointed.  I look forward to our brunches, but we'll just do it again next week, okay?

ALTHEA   Okay.  If you're sure.

ROBIN   I'm sure.  *(Beat)*   Who are you going with?

ALTHEA   *(Calmly)*   I told you, I don't want to talk abnout it right now.

ROBIN   Why not?

ALTHEA   Because I don't feel comfortable.  I'll talk to you tomorrow.

ROBIN   Why don't you feel comfortable.

ALTHEA   Because I don't.  Look, it's okay for you not to talk about why you're not mad at me.

ROBIN   I'm not mad at you.

ALTHEA   Then what are you?

ROBIN   I'm not anything.

ALTHEA   Well, you must be something, you're getting a little defensive.

ROBIN   I'm not getting defensive.  *(She is defensive.)*

ALTHEA   Then what are you?

ROBIN   *(She stares at her for a moment.)*   Althea, why don't you just go home, get up tomorrow morning, go on your bike date and then leave me alone. *(She exits SL into the bedroom.)*

ALTHEA   What did I say?

*(Lights out.)*


## SCENE TWO

*Lights up on* ROBIN'S *living room and kitchenette. It is the next morning. We can hear the sound of the vacuum being used in the bedroom along with a woman's voice singing ME AND BOBBY MCGEE. There is a knock at the door. The vacuuming and singing continue. there is another knock, louder this time and the door opens slowly. A woman sticks her head through the opening and says, "Hello, Robin?" She comes into the apartment and shuts the door. She calls loudly into the bedroom, "Robin?" No answer. "HELLO?" Still no answer. She's not sure what to do. She's uncomfortable being in the apartment because* ROBIN *doesn't know she's there, but she makes herself at home. She takes a couple of steps in and looks around the room. She notices some changes, but not many. Basically it's still the same apartment that she shared with* ROBIN *for two years. She walks over to the sofa and sits down, settling back. She is unable to get comfortable so she stands and crosses to the bookcase USR by the door and starts looking through books. Finally the vacuuming stops but the singing continues.* LESLIE *quickly puts back a book she has been glancing through as* ROBIN *walks into othe room carrying a dustrag.*

LESLIE   Hi.

ROBIN   Hi.

LESLIE   I tried to get your attention but you were busy. *(Points to bedroom.)*   You didn't hear me knock.  I hope you don't mind.

ROBIN   No, I'm just surprised.

LESLIE   I was going to call you, but I thought if I gave you a choice you might not see me.

ROBIN   I wasn't answering my phone anyway. *(They look at each other for a moment. It's an awkward but not unpleasant silence.)*

LESLIE   You haven't changed the apartment much.  I like the plants, they make the room look bigger somehow.

ROBIN   Do you want me to sit down?  Can I get you anything?  *(She crosses to the kitchenette to get rid of the dustrag.)*  I have some orange juice.

LESLIE   No, thanks.  I just ate.  I'm fine.

ROBIN   I think they just make it look more alive.  The plants.

LESLIE   Oh, yeah.  *(Beat)*   Look, about the party last night...

ROBIN   You didn't stay very long.

LESLIE   No, I didn't think you wanted me to.

ROBIN   Leslie, I told you that it was fine.  I really wouldn't have minded if you'd stayed.  I suppose if someone had told me before the party that you were going to be there with your new girlfriend...

LESLIE   She's not my girlfriend.  She was just a date.  We're just dating.

ROBIN   Everybody's dating these days.

LESLIE   I knew you thought she was my girlfriend.

ROBIN   It doesn't matter.  your date, your girlfriend, what's the difference?

LESLIE   The difference is I'm not seeing anybody seriously.

ROBIN   Oh.

LESLIE   I really miss you.

ROBIN   Well, I've missed you too.

LESLIE   Why haven't you called me?

ROBIN   You could have called me.

LESLIE   You told me you didn't want to see me.

ROBIN   Because you left.

LESLIE   You wanted me to leave.

ROBIN   I did not.  I wanted to work things out.

LESLIE   Yeah, your way.

ROBIN   Well, did you have a plan?  How did you want to work things out?

LESLIE   Okay, okay.  I didn't come over here to argue.  I realize things could have been different.  I'm sorry.

ROBIN   Yeah, me too.

LESLIE   So, you're still angry with me?

ROBIN   No, I'm not.  It just made me angry when you said I wanted you to leave. *(They are silent for a moment.)*   Maybe because it's partly true.  I wanted the you that I wanted you to be to stay.  But you stubbornly insisted on being the you you wanted to be.  I still don't understand that.  My version was much better.

LESLIE   How would you feel about giving me another chance to show you that my version's much better?

ROBIN   What?

LESLIE   Well, it's been six months.  Maybe we just needed some time off.

ROBIN   Time off?

LESLIE   Yeah, you know, to regroup.

ROBIN   Is that what you've been doing?

LESLIE   I don't know.  Maybe.  I'd like to find out.

ROBIN    You have an interesting way of regrouping.
She's very pretty.

LESLIE    I told you she was just a date.  Nothing serious.  After
I saw you, it was as if she wasn't even there.

ROBIN    I'll bet that made her feel really terrific.

LESLIE    You know what I mean.  Seeing you made me realize
how much I still care about you.

ROBIN    I still care about you, too.  I don't think that will ever
change.  But -

LESLIE    But what?

ROBIN    I haven't been regrouping.

LESLIE    Oh.

ROBIN    After you left, I didn't know what to do.  I don't think
I ever cried so much in my life.  I stayed out of work the first
couple of days because my face was so puffy.  I kept hoping
you'd call me - to tell me you'd made a mistake.  That you
couldn't live without me and you wanted to come back.  But you
didn't call me.  You went on with your life.  And finally I
realized I had a choice:  I could cling to the hope that someday
you'd come back and I would wait for you;  or I could be honest
with myself and let you go.

LESLIE    Well, I think I do want to come back.  I want us to
try again.

ROBIN    Leslie, what if you hadn't seen me at the party last night? Would you still be knocking on my door anyway today telling me you want us to try again?

LESLIE   I don't know.  That's not the point.

ROBIN   What is the point then?  That you've been thinking about me constantly for months.  That's why you've been seeing other women and haven't made one small effort to contact me until a day after you see me at a party where I'm obviously having a good time?

LESLIE   Why are you getting so angry?

ROBIN   Because you're too late.  You can't just come waltzing back into my life because you feel nostalgic.  And I think it takes a lot of nerve on your part to think you could walk in here and expect me to welcome you with open arms.

LESLIE   Look, I just thought.  I mean, I missed you.  I didn't come here to offend you or anything.

ROBIN   Well, it does offend me if you think I'm going to drop everything to be with you again.

LESLIE   Are you seeing someone?

ROBIN   That doesn't have anything to do with this.

LESLIE   So you are.

ROBIN   You know what, Leslie, this isn't a subject that I'm longing to discuss with you.   *(There is an awkward silence.)*

LESLIE   I guess it was pretty optimistic of me to think that you were still waiting for me. *(Gets up to leave.)* It's weird, but until now I've never actually thought of our relationship ending. But I guess I don't have a chance, huh?

ROBIN   You're the one who ended it.

LESLIE   I'm the one who left.

ROBIN   Yeah.

LESLIE   Well...(LESLIE *is at the door. She knows she is leaving but cannot bring herself to actually walk out the door.)* Are you still in therapy?

ROBIN   Yes, why?

LESLIE   I can tell. You say no really well.

ROBIN   Just one of my many unforeseen benefits.

LESLIE   *(Beat.)* Can I give you a hug before I go?

ROBIN   Sure. *(They hug.)*

LESLIE   Maybe I'll see you around.

ROBIN   Yeah.

LESLIE   Bye.

ROBIN   Bye. (ROBIN *shuts the door and then leans against it for a moment. She crosses to the kitchenette to retrieve her dustrag as the lights fade to black.)*

## SCENE THREE

*Lights up on an empty apartment. It is early afternoon. There is a knock at the door. Silence. There is another knock at the door.)*

ALTHEA *(Knocks again)* Robin? *(No answer. She tries the doorknob and opens the door.)* Robin?

ROBIN *(Enters)* I'm going to have to start locking my door.

ALTHEA *(Rather offended)* Sorry. Next time I'll just leave the flower on the welcome mat and go home. *(She is carrying a single flower which she gives to ROBIN.)*

ROBIN Thank you.

ALTHEA It's probably dead by now - the florist was out of those little water things they're supposed to put on the bottom. Do you mind if I sit down. *(She limps to the couch, sits, and gingerly puts her right leg up on the coffee table.)*

ROBIN *(Following ALTHEA to the couch.)* What happened? Why are you limping like that?

ALTHEA Why didn't you answer the door?

ROBIN I was cleaning. I didn't hear you.

ALTHEA *(This makes no sense to her)* You were cleaning, so you couldn't hear me?

ROBIN I was listening to some music at the same time, so I couldn't hear you.

ALTHEA   Oh, no wonder you didn't answer the phone earlier. I thought you were ignoring me, so I came over.

ROBIN   I did hear the phone.  I was ignoring you.  *(She gets up to put the flower in some water.)*

ALTHEA   Oh, hey Robin, don't feel like you have to protect my feelings.  Just come right out and say what's on your mind.

ROBIN   Well, I told you last night to leave me alone.  *(She's in the kitchenette)*  Do you want something to drink?

ALTHEA   It's up to you.  If you're going to ignore me, I'll go home right now, but if you're going to pay attention to me I'll have a soda.  *(ROBIN brings her a can of soda)*  Oh good, I get attention.  Good choice.

ROBIN   If you're going to gloat, I'll take back the soda and you can go home.

ALTHEA   I'm not gloating, I'm enjoying, I'm enjoying.  See? *(She takes a sip of soda)*  Hmm.  Very good.

ROBIN   What happened to your leg?

ALTHEA   I had a bad date?

ROBIN   *(Beat)*  Do you always come home limping from bad dates?

ALTHEA   No, only when I fall off bicycles.

ROBIN   Oh, Althea.  You fell off?

ALTHEA    Well, sort of.  More like nudged off.

ROBIN    Your date pushed you off your bicycle?

ALTHEA    No, not her.  I don't think I'm that masochistic.
Actually, she was very nice.  She apologized and everything, and
then took me to the emergency room.

ROBIN    She took you to the emergency room?  Althea, what
happened?  Why didn't you call me?  (ALTHEA *just looks at
her.*)  Oh right.  *(She looks at her with remorse.)*  Any stitches?

ALTHEA    Nine.

ROBIN    Nine stitches?

ALTHEA    They're just little stitches.  It's very neat.  It bled an
awful lot though.

ROBIN    Can I see it?

ALTHEA    You can't really see it.  It has a bandage on it.  *(She
tries to bunch her sweat pants over her knee, but it doesn't make
it.)*  Well, it's right here.  *(She shows* ROBIN *the exact spot on
her knee through the sweat pants.)*

ROBIN    Right here?  *(She very gingerly touches the sweat
pants over the bandage.* ALTHEA *sort of flinches, although it
does not hurt her.* ROBIN *slowly takes her hand away - it has
become an intimate moment.)*    Did that hurt?

ALTHEA    No, it was more the anticipation of pain.

ROBIN    *(She touches her leg again, only this time lower than the bandage.)*  Does it hurt here?  Are you bruised?

ALTHEA   No, just that one spot.  I'm perfectly fine everywhere else.

ROBIN   *(Takes her hand away.  She's enjoying touching ALTHEA, but is afraid she may be giving herself away.)*  So, who nudged you?

ALTHEA   Well, I don't think she really meant to nudge me.

ROBIN   Who's she?

ALTHEA   Barbara.

ROBIN   Barbara nudged you off the bicycle, but not on purpose, you don't think?

ALTHEA   Exactly.  you see we were waiting at a light and then the light turned green so I took my feet off the ground. That's when her bike hit my bike and I lost my balance.

ROBIN   And you fell and hit your knee.

ALTHEA   That's right.  Right on the curb.  Sliced it right in the middle on the fleshy part.  And her bike got sort of smashed up too.

ROBIN   Barbara fell off her bike too?

ALTHEA   No.

ROBIN   Then how did her bike get smashed up?

*237*

ALTHEA   I was riding it.

ROBIN   You were riding Barbara's bicycle?

ALTHEA   Yes.

ROBIN   Then whose bicycle was she riding anyway?

ALTHEA   Hers.  She has two.

ROBIN   Oh.  I see.  Who's Barbara?

ALTHEA   Chloe's ex.

ROBIN   Chloe's ex.  Who's Chloe?

ALTHEA   The woman I went riding with.

ROBIN   You went on a date with a woman and her ex lover?

ALTHEA   No, no, no.  Only with Chloe.

ROBIN   But Barbara was there.

ALTHEA   She showed up later.  She wasn't supposed to be there.

ROBIN   What did she do when you fell off the bicycle?

ALTHEA   Oh, she was mortified.  I told you, she took me to the emergency room.

ROBIN   No, I mean Barbara.

ALTHEA   Oh, she got pretty angry.

ROBIN   At herself.

ALTHEA   No, I hurt her bicycle.  Also, Chloe was paying a lot of attention to me.  I mean, I was bleeding quite a bit.

ROBIN   Are you going to see this woman again?

ALTHEA   No, I think she may get back together with Barbara.

ROBIN   The bicycle nudger?  You're kidding?

ALTHEA   No, I could tell that Chloe was kind of glad to see her.  They kept looking at each other.  You know.  Like this *(She looks at* ROBIN *as if there were no other woman in the world.)*  That kind of look.

ROBIN   Yeah.  I know that look.  *(She looks back at* ALTHEA.*)*

ALTHEA   Did Leslie look at you that way?

ROBIN   *(Looks away and shrugs.  She doesn't want to talk about* LESLIE.*)*  I guess so.  At the beginning.  But then Leslie looked at so many women like that.  I think it was the only look she had.

ALTHEA   Sorry.

ROBIN   There's nothing to be sorry for.  You didn't do anything.

ALTHEA   Sorry I brought it up.

ROBIN   Yeah, well...you know I -

ALTHEA *(At the same time)* - Do you think -

ROBIN   Oh, I'm sorry.  Go ahead.

ALTHEA   No, that's fine.  You go.

ROBIN   *(Beat)*   About last night?

ALTHEA   Yeah?

ROBIN   I really wasn't angry with you.

ALTHEA   No?

ROBIN   No.  You didn't do anything to make me angry.  I was just angry with me.

ALTHEA   Really?  What for?

ROBIN   *(This is difficult for her.)*   Well, hmmm.  I just don't...you know when you become friends with somebody and you get to know them really well and sometimes they turn out to be ...ah...*(She stops.  She's not ready yet.  She gets up.)*   Do you want something else to drink?

ALTHEA   No.  I'm fine.

ROBIN   I'll be right back. *(She crosses to kitchenette and gets herself something to drink from the refrigerator.)*  How do you date?

ALTHEA   What do you mean?

ROBIN   You seem to do it so well.  I've always been under the impression that lesbians can't date.  They cohabitate.

ALTHEA   Well, it's a learned thing.  You have to have very specific rules in order for it to work.

ROBIN   Really?  What are they?  *(She comes back into the living room.)*

ALTHEA   Are you planning to date someone?

ROBIN   It depends on what the rules are.

ALTHEA   There isn't a rule book.  You make them up yourself.  It's whatever you're comfortable with.

ROBIN   What works for you?

ALTHEA   Okay.  My two basic rules are:  only date women you want to be friends with, and no sex.  But depending on the situation those rules can change.

ROBIN   If they change, then how can they be rules?

ALTHEA   See, that's what I mean.  You have to scope out the situation first, based on those two rules and then you need to be flexible.

ROBIN   Doesn't sound very specific to me.

ALTHEA   Oh, but it is.  The rules depend on the specific person you're with.

ROBIN   How can you have two basic rules that then change

based on who you're with?

ALTHEA   I think you're missing the point.  Those are the two
rules for dating.  Then they change when you're not dating
anymore.

ROBIN   I'm confused.

ALTHEA   You see, the dating period is the time when you get
to know somebody.  It's the process in which you divide people
into categories.  Just friends, flings, affairs, and lovers.  Then
there are the specific rules you follow within those categories.

ROBIN   This is a pretty elaborate system.  What's the
difference between a fling and an affair?

ALTHEA   A fling is someone you just want to be friends with
and she just wants to be friends with you and you're both very
clear about that.  But there's a little sexual tension between you
that you want to explore.  So you have sex.  And it's usually
okay, but it isn't great - which is what you've suspected all along
and then when that's over you move into the just friends
category.  An affair is someone you  have sex with who you are
incredibly attracted to.  It usually lasts until one partner starts to
expect more than just sex.  Or until both partners expect more
than just sex.  Then you become lovers.

ROBIN   God, it's so clinical.  You sound like a sociologist.
What about feelings?  Where's the falling in love part?

ALTHEA   Gees, Robin, you asked me about dating, not about
falling in love.

ROBIN   Don't you ever fall in love with the people you're dating?

*242*

ALTHEA   Every now and then.  That's why there's a lovers category.  But that's a whole different story.

ROBIN   I feel like I've just read THE SECRET LIFE OF PLANTS.  I can't believe you have all those categories.

ALTHEA   Yeah, but people don't usually fit so neatly into them.  They mix and match.  Depending on who they are and how you feel about them and how they feel about you.  Actually, sometimes it gets pretty messy.  That's why you have a dating period, so you can avoid the messy parts.

ROBIN   What category does Chloe fit into?

ALTHEA   The not ready to be anything because she's confused category.

ROBIN   You could write a book.  LESBIANS WHO DATE AND THE WOMEN WHO LOVE THEM.

ALTHEA   More likely LESBIANS WHO TRY TO DATE AND THE WOMEN WHO HATE THEM.  *(They are companionably silent for a moment.)*

ROBIN   How about the women who are friends for a long time first who want to do more than date?

ALTHEA   You'll have to write your own book.

ROBIN   So you've never had a relationship with one of your friends?

ALTHEA   But that's the point of dating:  you get to know each other and become friends.

ROBIN   *(Realizing this line of questioning is not working.)*
Look, Althea, about last night.

ALTHEA   Yeah?

ROBIN   Well, I just need to tell you this so that it doesn't ruin
our friendship.

ALTHEA   Okay.

ROBIN   Okay. *(She stops. She's in danger of not being able
to continue once again.)*  This is so hard.  Why is this so hard?
Okay.  I've always been very clear about our relationship.  We've
always been good friends.  I mean, one of us has always been in
a good relationship since our friendship began, so it's like, never
been a question for me.  But now that you're doing this dating
thing, which obviously doesn't work all the time, and I've been
single for almost six months, well...*(she stops for a moment
searching for the right words)*  my heart has been doing different
things. *(She now realizes that that sounded strange and rather
vague.)*  I mean, ah...not only my heart but my whole body.
Yeah, it's a whole body thing too.  Gees, I feel like such an
idiot.  Okay, what I mean to say is that for some time now, I'm
not exactly sure how long because I don't think I wanted to
notice it at first, I've been attracted to you. *(She cannot look at
ALTHEA while she is saying this because she wants to get the
whole thing out - she is standing up - perhaps pacing back and
forth, trying not only to get it clear for ALTHEA but also for
herself.)*  I haven't said anything before this because I thought it
might go away.  I mean, Leslie and I had just broken up and I
was afraid maybe I was trying to avoid facing that.  Also, God,
Althea, we have the best friendship, I've never been able to -
blah - be myself so completely before.  You don't run away no
matter what I say to you.  You just keep coming back.  That's

244

nice, I like that. I didn't want to ruin that, don't want to ruin that - am I ruining that? *(She finally looks at* ALTHEA *but continues on before she gets an answer.)* Anyway, after last night I knew for sure that it wouldn't go away - that the feeling was real and that it had nothing to do with Leslie. And I got really angry with myself because, damn, I don't want to be in - I mean, I don't want you to go away from me. *(She is exhausted. She sits on the couch as far away from* ALTHEA *as possible.)* Anyway, I wanted to tell you that so that it wouldn't get in the way of what we have. Okay, I feel better now, it's out in the open. *(Silence. They both sit there for a moment.)* No, no. Now I feel worse. Are you just going to sit there and not say anything? At least, I know you can't run screaming from the room. You'd have to limp slowly.

ALTHEA   Why did you suddenly realize this last night?

ROBIN   Leslie was at the party last night.

ALTHEA   She was? I didn't see her.

ROBIN   No, she didn't stay. She came through the door with this woman I'd never seen before. She was very pretty. I knew that sooner or later I would eventually see Leslie with another woman. You know how you picture the worse possible thing that could happen - sometimes it would strike me at the strangest moments. I'd go into a public restroom and suddenly panic with the thought that Leslie would be in there with some woman and I'd interrupt them - how embarrassing, how humiliating - I would just die. I hoped that I would die so they would feel tremendous guilt and never be able to have a happy relationship together. It was this nightmare that used to follow me everywhere I went at first. That's why I didn't go out for a long time. It was that fear. Then eventually the fear went away and I didn't even notice it leave. Then when I saw her at the party last night holding hands with that other woman - all the fear came back to me and I waited for that terrible pain to happen to my heart. The pain that makes your knees weak and your breath short, and your head kind of dizzy. And I deliberately looked straight at them willing this pain to come, almost daring it to happen - and then Leslie saw me. And her mouth sort of opened - you know that saying that her jaw dropped open - it really did - it was kind of funny, I'd never actually seen that happen. And she let go of the woman's hand like she felt guilty or something. Then she walked right over to me and said, 'Hi, you look beautiful. Can I have a hug?' And you know how in movies they have these moments where everything happens in slow motion and nothing exists except those two people in the scene - well there I was expecting this pain to happen - I was waiting and waiting for it - and then she hugged me and I guess I hugged her back I can't remember - and then wham! I realized that the pain was over, it was never going to come. I didn't care tht she was at this party with another woman and I didn't care that she thought I was beautiful. I was stunned. I almost felt cheated - the drama was over, and I hadn't even known it. Then she said, 'Do you mind we're here? Do you want us to leave?' And I said, 'Leslie, you can do what you want. I don't care.' Well, she left pretty quickly anyway. Her date seemed sort of irritated and kept looking at me out of the corner of her eye. I pretended I didn't notice. As they were going out of the door, Leslie waved to me and I waved back and that was it. No pain. Nothing. And I thought, wow, therapy really does help. I take back all the whining I did about spending that money.

ALTHEA    Why didn't you tell me this happened?

ROBIN    Well, I was going to. I went looking for you. But you were in the corner flirting with some blond woman who was

ROBIN   Well, I was going to.  I went looking for you.  But you were in the corner flirting with some blond woman who was hanging all over you.

ALTHEA   She was not HANGING all over me.

ROBIN   She had her arms around your neck.

ALTHEA   That isn't hanging.  She was just being friendly.

ROBIN   No, being friendly is touching an arm, or perhaps hugging you quickly and letting you go.  This was definitely hanging.

ALTHEA   I didn't even know her.

ROBIN   Well, it certainly looked like you knew her.

ALTHEA   Why didn't you tell me when we got home?

ROBIN   I was mad at you.

ALTHEA   You were MAD at me?

ROBIN   Yes.  Here I was having all of those emotional upheavals and you were off in some corner flirting with a woman you didn't even know.

ALTHEA   But you said you weren't mad at me.  Several times.

ROBIN   Well, I was alright?  But I didn't have any right to be. It made me mad that I was mad at you.  How can we be friends if I get mad at you everytime you make eyes at someone?

ROBIN   Why?

ALTHEA   You tell me all these things - you tell me how you feel about me - and you don't even ask how I feel about you - or even what I think about how you feel about me.

ROBIN   Well, I just assumed.

ALTHEA   Assumed what?

ROBIN   That you just wanted to be friends.  You said I'd have to write the book.

ALTHEA   What book?

ROBIN   You know, the one about women being friends for a long time and then wanting to be more than just friends.

ALTHEA   It doesn't mean I don't want to READ the book.

ROBIN   *(Flustered)*  Oh *(Beat)*  Do you want to read the book?

ALTHEA   I want to do more than read the book.  I want to take its advice.

ROBIN   *(Still flustered)*  Oh.  Really?

ALTHEA   Really.

ROBIN   I feel kind of...I don't know what the advice would be. *(Silence)*  You're not going to help me are you?  (ALTHEA *shakes her head no.*)  Okay.  Why not?

ALTHEA   Because I'm not good at dating.  I'm not so sure

about being in love.

ROBIN   Is that what you are?

ALTHEA   Is that what YOU are?

ROBIN   I asked you first.

ALTHEA   Robin.  You started this.

ROBIN   You're right.  Okay.  Yes.

ALTHEA   Yes?

ROBIN   Yes, I'm in love with you.

ALTHEA   Really.  Wow.  I thought I'd never hear you say it.
I've been feeling that way for a long time.

ROBIN   You're kidding.  How long?

ALTHEA   *(She thinks for a moment.)*   Since before Leslie.

ROBIN   Why didn't you say anything?

ALTHEA   Well, my relationship with Chris was ending, not
because of you, and I didn't want to jump into another
relationship.  Then you met Leslie.

ROBIN   But then Leslie and I broke up.

ALTHEA   And then you were getting over Leslie.

ROBIN   God, you are so healthy.  I wouldn't have been able to

*249*

keep my mouth shut. I would have told you immediately and ruined everything.

ALTHEA   But you didn't tell me right away. You did wait.

ROBIN   Yeah, well, three years ago I wasn't in therapy. *(They look at each other. They are silent for a few moments.)* So what next?

ALTHEA   I don't know. What's next?

ROBIN   How about a bike ride? No? What about a hug?

ALTHEA   That I think I can manage. *(They awkwardly hug.)* The physical distance between friends and lovers is a long one.

ROBIN   *(Still embracing)*   Is this okay? How's your knee?

ALTHEA   My knee?

ROBIN   The one with the nine stitches in it?

ALTHEA   I don't know. Maybe you should take a look at it.

ROBIN   You'd have to take these off. *(Indicates sweat pants.)*

ALTHEA   I know. *(Beat)*

ROBIN   Althea?

ALTHEA   Yeah?

ROBIN   Do you ever get scared?

ALTHEA   All the time.

ROBIN   Good.  I don't want it to be just me.  *(She gets up and crosses to the door.)*

ALTHEA   What are you doing?

ROBIN   Locking the door.  *(She locks the door and crosses back to* ALTHEA *on the couch.)*   Now let's take a look at that knee.  *(She sits down and leans in to kiss* ALTHEA *as the lights go dark.)*

◆◆◆◆◆◆◆◆◆◆◆◆◆◆◆◆◆◆◆◆◆◆◆◆◆◆◆◆◆◆◆◆◆◆◆

PAM CADY has been involved in the theatre since the fifth grade when she played CLARA in THE NUTCRACKER, and in the overexcitement of the moment, she hit the Nutcracker over the head with her slipper instead of the Mouseking.  Since then, she has collected an M.F.A. in Acting from California State University in Long Beach.  There she met her lover, Suzanne, an artist, with whom she now resides with their five year old daughter, Julian. This playwright-actor-singer-acting teacher and director says, "I've been around the theatre all my life; now I manage a very cool bookstore.  I live happily with my lover and our daughter.  We work very hard at being good parents to her."  She adds, "We are in the process of trying to sell our house to move to some picturesque and lesbian-friendly spot in the Pacific Northwest."

PAM CADY

# EBONY LOVE
## by Lynn Emidia


My love loves jelly beans
She carries them round
in her worn out jeans

Red ones
Yellow ones
Green ones too

But the black ones
Are the ones
With which I woo

Her eyes will twinkle
With each licorice drop
She'll neatly
Sweetly
Pop

       Pop

          Pop

Breakfast
Dinner
Luncheon too

My love
Even eats
Jelly bean stew

# *Portrait of Ellen Symons*

**Self Portrait: for Louise I  1992          Photo by Ellen Symons**

**Self Portrait:  for Louise III   1992          Photo by Ellen Symons**

Ellen Symons - "I am a thirty-one year old, white, middle-class
lesbian poet, artist and activist, (now living in Ontario, Canada)
looking at life through the lens of an anti-racist, feminist...
vegetarian dyke.  I have had poems and stories published in a few
magazines and in one anthology, GETTING WET:TALES OF
LESBIAN SEDUCTIONS, Toronto:  Women's Press, 1992, and
have recently started working more seriously with photographs...

*Photos by Ellen Symons*

254

*Photos by Ellen Symons*

...It's the details of things, the nooks and crannies, that capture my imagination. Photography is new to me, and satisfying - it gives me a lot of scope to explore."

255

*Lori and Nari    Photography by Ana R. Kissed*